FERGUSON
CAREER BIOGRAPHIES

STEPHEN
KING

Author

James Robert Parish

Ferguson
An imprint of ☑®Facts On File

Stephen King: Author

Copyright © 2005 by Facts On File, Inc.

Ferguson
An imprint of Facts On File, Inc.
132 West 31st Street
New York NY 10001

Library of Congress Cataloging-in-Publication Data
Parish, James Robert.
   Stephen King—author / by James Robert Parish.
      p. cm
   Includes bibliographical references (p.   ) and index.
   ISBN 0-8160-5543-2 (acid-free paper)
   1. King, Stephen, 1947—Juvenile literature. 2. Novelists, American—20th century—Biography—Juvenile literature 3. Horror tales—Authorship—Juvenile literature.
[1. King, Stephen, 1947– 2. Authors, American.] I. Title: Stephen King. II. Title.
   PS3561.I483Z785 2004
   813'.54—dc22   2003028013

Ferguson books are available at special discounts when purchased in bulk quantities for businesses, associations, institutions, or sales promotions. Please call our Special Sales Department in New York at (212) 967-8800 or (800) 322-8755.

You can find Ferguson on the World Wide Web at http://www.fergpubco.com

Text design by David Strelecky

Pages 111–129 adapted from *Ferguson's Encyclopedia of Careers and Vocational Guidance, Twelfth Edition*

Printed in the United States of America

MP Hermitage 10 9 8 7 6 5 4 3 2 1

CONTENTS

1

AMERICA'S MOST POPULAR WRITER

In late 2003, Stephen King was awarded the Medal for Distinguished Contribution to American Letters at the National Book Awards. This prestigious literary prize seems only fitting for today's most popular living novelist. King's books have sold many millions of copies over recent decades, have been translated into 33 different languages, and have been published in over 35 countries. Like much in King's life, however, this professional achievement did not come easily or without its share of controversy.

King, often called the "Steven Spielberg of horror" and "America's favorite boogeyman," first gained fame with his debut novel, *Carrie* (1974). Since then, he has been known as a highly commercial writer who deftly turns out best-selling fiction, especially in the horror genre. (A genre is a specific writing category; romance, science fiction, and mystery are other genres.) Adding to King's renown is that many of his works have been adapted into feature films and TV miniseries. His talents have won the praise of fellow genre writers, including well-regarded author/filmmaker Clive Barker, who observes of King, "I think his genius is to make horror acceptable. . . ." According to Barker, Stephen "turned the horror genre—so long an underdog on the publishing scene—into a force to be reckoned with."

But Stephen King has struggled long to gain respectability within the publishing industry. Some consider his books to be merely entertaining reading for the masses rather than artistic achievements with any real literary merit. The famed author has acknowledged his fight to gain legitimacy with his peers: "When I was young, I used to think it should be easy to wed popular fiction with literary fiction. But as time went by and I got older, I began to realize how difficult it really is. I began to realize how many people are so set against it."

Nevertheless, millions of readers around the globe relish King's stories, prizing his abilities as a master storyteller. They seem unmindful that his prose may not be in the same higher artistic league of such National Book Awards winners as Toni Morrison, Philip Roth, Arthur Miller, and John Updike. In *Landscape of Fear: Stephen King's American Gothic* (1988), Tony Magistrale offers one explanation for Stephen's popularity: "King's best work employs many of the same techniques found in film. . . He possesses the ability to maintain levels of suspense because the imaginary world he portrays is so accurately visual."

Over the years, King's many published writings have covered and intermingled literary genres. However, he is best known for such chilling fiction as *'Salem's Lot* (1976), *The Shining* (1977), and *Pet Sematary* (1983), all of which strikingly emphasize elements of the supernatural. In his horror stories, Stephen successfully follows in the literary tradition of famous authors such as Mary Shelley, Nathaniel Hawthorne, Edgar Allan Poe, and H. P. Love-craft.

From early childhood, and from the start of his writing career, overly imaginative Stephen was drawn to tales of the horrific because they hold the "ability to form a liaison between our fantasy fears and our real fears." He also appreciates why people like to be scared: "There are some people whose lives are full of fears—that their marriage isn't working, that they aren't going to make it on the job, that society is crumbling all around them." According to

Stephen King delivers his address at the 2003 National Book Awards, where he received the Medal for Distinguished Contribution to American Letters. (Associated Press)

King, because most people are too timid to deal with or even discuss such matters with others, they lack "outlets for all those scary feelings. . . . The horror writer can give them a place to put their fears, and it's OK to be afraid then, because nothing is real, and you can blow it all away when it's over."

As an expert in his literary genre, King has found three ways to scare his readers. "Naturally, I'll try to terrify you first, and if that doesn't work, I'll try to horrify you, and if I can't make it there, I'll try to gross you out." But this remarkable ability to grab the reader's attention is only one aspect of Stephen's tremendous success as an author. According to *The Encyclopedia of World Biography* (1998), "King's wide popularity attests to his ability to create stories in which he emphasizes the inability to rationalize certain facets of evil in seemingly commonplace situations." In short, King has a knack that all great storytellers possess—the ability to greatly entertain a wide range of readers with his compelling and exciting fiction.

2

HUMBLE BEGINNINGS

Stephen Edwin King was born on September 21, 1947, at the General Hospital in Portland, Maine. The future novelist was the second child of Donald, a vacuum-cleaner salesman, and his wife, Nellie Ruth Pillsbury King, a homemaker. The family lived modestly in Scarborough, a little town about eight miles south of Portland. Two years earlier, when the Kings thought they were unable to have their own children, they had adopted a newborn infant, whom they named David Victor King.

Donald King had been in the Merchant Marines during World War II. He had served on vessels that ferried people and supplies for the military. Not long after Stephen's birth, Donald resigned from the Merchant Marines. He found it difficult to readjust to civilian life, however, and restlessly switched from job to job. When Stephen was two years old, Mr. King one day said he was going out to the grocery store to buy a package of cigarettes. He never returned. This desertion left lifelong emotional scars on the King family.

Suddenly a single parent of two youngsters, Ruth King had to become the sole support of the household. Although she was distantly related to the wealthy Pillsbury baking fortune, she had no savings of her own and needed to earn an income—immediately. With ex-servicemen crowding the job market in the post-World War II era, however, it was difficult for women to find decent jobs. Moreover, her work experience did not lend itself easily to securing employment in small-town Maine.

Until Ruth could find work, she called upon her sisters to help with the boys. For a time, Stephen went to stay with his aunt Ethelyn and her husband, Oren, in Durham, Maine at their farmhouse. David, now four, was sent to his Aunt Molly's in Malden, Massachusetts. Within a few months, Mrs. King had scraped together enough money from an assortment of jobs that required minimal skill to be able to reunite with her children.

Childhood Moves

Over the next four years, Ruth King and her boys were frequently on the move. They stayed with Donald King's mother in Chicago for a while. Later, they were taken in by relatives in West De Pere, Wisconsin, followed by a brief stay in Texas. Later, they relocated to Fort Wayne, Indiana, where Ruth's sister-in-law, a schoolteacher, took them into her home. To pay their way during this difficult period, Ruth worked various jobs, including housekeeper, laundry presser, and doughnut maker. When Mrs. King was hired at a local General Electric plant in Fort Wayne, winding coils for small motors, she and her sons moved into their own apartment.

At age four, Stephen suffered a traumatic experience. One day Stephen returned home with his face deathly pale and his pants damp from having wet himself. He immediately went to his room, where he remained alone for hours, refusing to talk with his concerned mother. Ruth later discovered the reason for Stephen's sudden somberness. He had been playing with a neighborhood friend who had been run over by a freight train on a nearby railroad line. She now understood the horrified look that had been on Stephen's face. She knew that he had witnessed his pal being torn apart by the passing train. However, to the present day, King's only recollection of the horrendous event is what his mother told him much later—that the boy's remains were picked up in a wicker basket and taken for burial. This tragedy, as with so many other events in King's life, provided a basis for one of Stephen's future stories. His pal's grotesque death was worked into "The Body," which was published in the 1982 collection *Different Seasons* and was adapted into the 1986 feature film *Stand by Me.*

Not long before Stephen's sixth birthday, the Kings moved yet again, this time to Stratford, Connecticut, where Ruth's sister Gert lived. Once Mrs. King found work (in a laundry), they moved into their own apartment. By now, David was in the fourth grade (having begun schooling before his fifth birthday and having

The young stars of the film Stand by Me *(1986). The film is based on the novella* The Body, *which was inspired by a traumatic event from Stephen's childhood.* (Photofest)

skipped the second grade) and Stephen was entering kindergarten.

During the often difficult years that Ruth King and her sons had moved about the country, she taught her children to appreciate the simple pleasures of life. One of her great joys was reading: She always had a stack of inexpensive paperbacks lying about the house. She called these books "a pile of cheap, sweet vacations." She passed on her deep love of literature to her boys.

A good deal of Stephen's sixth year was spent in bed, coping with painful tonsillitis and serious ear infections. To pass the long days, he devoured comic books. (One of his favorites was *Tales from the Crypt*.) To amuse himself, he began to write down the story lines from these comics on note paper. One evening, he showed one of his "writings" to his mother. While she praised his initiative, she suggested, "Write one of your own, Stevie. . . . I bet you could do better."

Stephen was inspired by his mother's suggestion of writing his own story. As he has described, "I remember an immense feeling of possibility at the idea, as if I had been ushered into a vast building filled with closed doors and had been given leave to open any I liked." Before too long, the youngster had composed a short story (four pages of handwriting) in which he told of a bunny rabbit that had the unusual ability to drive a car. Stephen's mother insisted that the tale was worthy of publication. Years later, Stephen admitted, "Nothing anyone has said to me since has made me feel any happier."

Stephen continued with his story writing. He discovered to his amazement and great pleasure that in creating stories he could devise his own universe(s) and control his cast of characters. As King later explained, "Once you get a taste of that kind of power, you're lost forever."

The Developing Creative Artist

In addition to his mother's encouragement, several other things served as imaginative stimuli for Stephen's budding talent. When Stephen was seven, he was especially intrigued by one of the books his mother had just checked out of the library. The volume was *The Strange Case of Dr. Jekyll and Mr. Hyde,* by Robert Louis Stevenson. The curious youngster wanted to know more about the story. After his mother told him a few details of the mild-mannered scientist/doctor who turns himself into a savage individual, he asked her to read him the full story. She insisted it was too scary for a child his age. Stephen persisted, however, and his mother finally gave in—reading him the remarkable narrative. It made a great impression on the highly imaginative boy. Said King, "I lived and died with that story. . . . I can remember lying in bed, wakeful after that night's reading was done."

That same year, Ruth took David and Stephen to a local drive-in theater. While David slept in the car, Stephen sat engrossed at *The Creature from the Black Lagoon* (1954). It was his first horror film, and he never forgot the exciting experience. While the youngster appreciated that what he was viewing was make-believe and that the frightening title figure was nothing more than an actor in a rubber suit, it stimulated his highly active imagination.

After seeing *The Creature from the Black Lagoon*, Stephen envisioned the possibility of such a creature coming to his house and hiding in the shadows, or in the closet, or under the bed, ready to claim the seven-year old as his latest victim. Such vivid speculations were a constant source of entertainment and terror to the boy who spent so much of his time playing out ghoulish stories in his mind.

This fright movie also sparked Stephen to write his first real horror story. It was about a dinosaur that terrified a town. A scientist uncovers that the terrorizing beast has a strong aversion to anything leather. Utilizing this knowledge, the townsfolk taunt the beast with assorted leather items, until finally it leaves.

Before long, Stephen was turning out such fanciful stories frequently, partially inspired by his Aunt Gert, who gave him a reward for each of his efforts. She paid nine-

The Creature from the Black Lagoon *(1954), the first horror film Stephen ever saw, provided the inspiration for his first horror story.* (Photofest)

year-old King a quarter for his fairy tale, "Jhonathan and the Witches." In that narrative, the hero kills a trio of witches and lives happily ever after with his dad. (Years later, in 1993, this story would be reprinted in *First Words*, a collection of early writings by well-known authors.) In writing "Jhonathan and the Witches" and reading many fairy tales (e.g., *The 500 Hats of Bartholomew Cubbins*, by Dr. Seuss), the youngster soon discovered that these seemingly harmless children's stories often contained strange, unpredictable, and scary plot twists. For a boy with Stephen's heightened imagination and sense of fear, reading and writing such scary pieces was a pivotal point for his later career as a master of horror fiction.

Apart from the Crowd

At school, Stephen felt like the odd boy out. He earned good grades, but because he was tall for his age (he was the oldest in his class), pudgy, and wore glasses, his classmates considered him something of a geek. When the other kids played sports, awkward and clumsy King was generally the last picked for any team.

As an escape from his unsettled childhood, King spent a lot of time by himself reading. Because the family could not afford to buy many books, Stephen frequented the local library. He also found great delight in listening to the radio (no one in his family or circle had a TV set at the time), especially to science-fiction and horror programs. He also had a great enthusiasm for rock and roll music and was thrilled when his mother gave him an Elvis Presley record for Christmas. Stephen played the record over and over until it wore out.

King was a regular moviegoer as well, whenever he and his brother could afford the price of admission. Their preferences were horror and science-fiction pictures. After the show, Stephen often rushed home and wrote his own adaptation of the story he had just witnessed on screen.

In October 1957 Stephen was watching a Saturday matinee performance of *Earth vs. the Flying Saucers* at the local cinema. Partway through the film, the picture stopped, the house lights went on, and the annoyed audience started booing. The manager rushed to the front of the auditorium, where he nervously announced that the Russians had just launched *Sputnik I* into outer space. Most of the patrons—especially the kids—didn't want to accept that the Soviets had suddenly jumped ahead of America in the space race, but King understood that it was true. When the movie about aliens attacking the Earth resumed, Stephen was immediately struck by the parallels of movie fiction and the realities of technology in the late 1950s. He has also said of this indelible experience, "I still find it impossible to convey, even to my own kids, how terribly frightened and alone and depressed I felt at that moment."

Shaping His Future

In 1958, when Stephen was 11, Mrs. King and her two children moved to Durham, Maine. It had been arranged between Ruth and her siblings that if she would take care of their aged parents, they would provide her and the boys with a house to live in and the basic necessities. As such, they settled into a very modest two-story house next to the West Durham United Methodist Church (where the family attended services and the boys attended Bible class) and close to the home of Aunt Evelyn and Uncle Oren. The Kings' old-fashioned new dwelling relied on water from a well in the yard. Their bathroom was an outhouse at the back of the property. Taking a shower in wintertime proved to be a tricky business. The boys used the facilities at their relatives' and then rushed back home through the cold.

Despite the hardships of their daily existence, Ruth, as always, continued to be upbeat and to show her children how much she loved them. In acknowledging his mother's ongoing struggle to keep the family together in a loving environment, Stephen observes, "I was a hell of a lot less deprived than countless children of middle-class or wealthy families, whose parents have time for everything but their kids."

Stephen attended grade school at a one-room school-house down the road from where he lived. In his new environment, his height, pudginess, thick glasses, and gawkiness again condemned him to being an outsider in the classroom and when it came time for his peers to choose teams for games.

Stephen increasingly escaped into his imagination by reading and writing. His mother had come across an old Underwood typewriter (which boasted a few broken letters), and the young King learned to type his stories. His 13-year-old brother also liked to write and began self-publishing a newspaper, *Dave's Rag*. The first edition, in January 1959, had a print run of two copies and was typed on the family's Underwood. By that April, the circulation had risen to 20 copies and was selling for a nickel. David was the editor-in-chief/illustrator, with Stephen as reporter, and their cousin Donald P. Flaws as sports editor. Before the venture eventually ended, *Dave's Rag* was turned out on an old mimeograph machine that Ruth had found.

In *Dave's Rag* Stephen ran ads offering his stories for sale. Seeking a wider marketplace, he attempted to market his fiction at school. Once, after seeing *The Pit and the Pendulum* (1961), a film adaptation of a classic Edgar Allan Poe story, he typed his own eight-page version of the fright tale. He sold copies to classmates at 25 cents each. Sales were running briskly until the principal, Miss Hisler, intervened and made him return the money, insisting school was not the place for such transactions.

She also reprimanded Stephen for his prose. She said, "What I don't understand, Stevie, is why you'd write junk like this in the first place. You're talented; why do you want to waste your abilities?" King admits the rebuke had a long-lasting effect: "I was ashamed. I have spent a good many years since—too many, I think—being ashamed about what I write."

A Remarkable Discovery

One autumn afternoon around 1960, while Stephen and David were investigating boxes in their aunt's cluttered attic, they came across a gathering of items that had belonged to the boys' father. In the midst of the dust-covered box were old paperback novels and magazines (demonstrating that Stephen inherited his love of horrific tales from his dad) as well as rejection slips from bygone times when Donald King had submitted his own stories to magazines for possible publication. (While Stephen never found or got to read any of his dad's writings, it made him feel a bit closer to this man, who long ago had disappeared from his life.)

Also in the collection of keepsakes was an eight-millimeter home movie shot during World War II while Mr. King was in the Merchant Marines. The boys were anxious to see footage of their dad, whom David vaguely remembered and Stephen never really knew. The brothers scraped together enough money to rent a projector and view the footage.

Regarding the experience, King says, "After we'd gone through a couple of reels of film, David jumped up and said, 'That's him! That's our father!' He'd [Mr. King] handed the camera to one of his buddies and there he was, lounging against a ship's rail, a choppy sea in the background. My old man . . . He raised his hand and smiled, unwittingly waving at sons who weren't born yet. 'Hi, Dad, don't forget to write.'"

It was a mixed blessing for Stephen to have this reunion with the dad who had deserted him years before, leaving such emptiness and anger in his life. In later years, he would refer to his father (infrequently) only in abrupt, unkind words about the many hardships he had caused his wife and children.

3

FINDING INSPIRATION

By age 13, enterprising Stephen King was already mailing off his latest short stories for publication consideration by such science-fiction magazines as *Fantastic* and *The Magazine of Fantasy and Science Fiction*. His submissions did not meet with success with the publishers, but he refused to become discouraged. He continued sending his work, which, in turn, added to his pile of rejection slips from the publications. As a reminder that he must always keep trying his craft, he skewered the slips to a nail on his bedroom wall. According to the determined novice writer, "By the time I was 14 . . . the nail in my wall would no longer support all the weight of rejection slips impaled upon it. I replaced the nail with a spike and went on writing."

The teenager graduated from secondary school (in a class of three) in the spring of 1962. Because Durham was too small to have its own high school, Stephen had to commute six miles away to Lisbon Falls High School. Academically, Stephen did well with subjects that incorporated writing. In contrast, he had no knack for physics or chemistry, and his grades in those sciences showed it. Once again, in his class, big-boned King was the tallest student (soon reaching his full height of six feet, four inches), still chunky and buck-toothed, and continued to wear thick glasses. He often felt "unhappy and different." As he described, "My high school career was totally undistinguished. I was not at the top of my class, nor at the bottom." He acknowledged, "I had friends, but none of them were the big jocks or the student council guys or anything like that."

One of Stephen's best pals at the time was Chris Chesley, a neighbor from Durham. They shared a common love of writing. They also had similar tastes in fiction, admiring the writings of Richard Matheson and Don Robertson. Chris realized the special artistic abilities of his friend, who he envisioned would have a promising writing career. Chesley has said, "When I went to Stephen King's house to write stories with him, there was the sense that these things weren't just stories; when you walked inside the walls of his house, there was a sense of palpability, almost as if the characters in the stories had real weight. . . . Imagination didn't just make it real for him—it made it real for me." Further, according to Chris, "When you read stories with him, or read his writing, or participated and wrote stories with him, [it became] a world unto itself, and I was privileged to enter it. Even as a kid, a teenager, King had the power to do that. It was an amazing thing."

Stephen and Chris also made a haunted house movie, using the eight-millimeter camera that Mrs. King had given her older boy. In addition, the two youths explored the local cemetery, carefully studying the tombstones and wondering why the graveyard contained so many markers for people who had died so young. (Such speculation would turn up in King's later writings, including 1983's *Pet Sematary*.)

The Avid Reader and Writer

If Stephen was not a remarkable scholar at Lisbon Falls High, he was well known to his classmates as a passionate reader, one who always carried a paperback in the back pocket of his worn jeans. Among his preferred authors at the time were Ray Bradbury, Ken Kesey, Ed McBain, John D. MacDonald, Shirley Jackson, and, a favorite from his boyhood, Jack London.

As an outsider, King developed a unique way of looking at the world around him. From his viewpoint, conformity should be regarded with suspicion. He also believed that nonconformists would get their payback against the world in unique ways. Later, he admitted, "At times, particularly in my teens, I felt violent, as if I wanted to lash out at the world, but that rage I kept hidden. That was a secret place I wouldn't reveal to anyone else."

Tied into Stephen's special outlook on life was that as an extremely trusting youth who too quickly believed most things he was told, he had many

Stephen King has always been an avid reader. (Photofest)

fears and was very superstitious. As he told *Time* magazine in an October 1986 cover story, his fears included "spiders, elevators, closed-in-places, the dark, sewers, funerals, the ideas of being buried alive, cancer, heart attacks, the number 13, black cats and walking under ladders."

Stephen's nonconformity and gleeful sense of the absurd led him to self-publish a parody of his school's newspaper. Entitled *The Village Vomit*, the satirical underground offering poked fun at, among other topics, several of Lisbon Falls High's teachers.

Stephen's unorthodox creativity got an immediate response—not one he appreciated. As soon as *The Village Vomit* began circulating, Stephen was ordered to report to the principal's office at the close of the school day. There it was decided that he must apologize to the teachers he had offended and spend a week in detention class. In addition, the high school's guidance counselor added another chore for King's repentance. He arranged for the teenager to become a sportswriter at the *Lisbon Enterprise*. Writing for the local publication, Stephen would receive a half cent per printed word when his articles were published.

As the guidance counselor had intended, working under John Gould, editor of the *Lisbon Enterprise*, was a rewarding experience. King has said, "I protested that I didn't know anything about sports and the guy says, 'Do you know how to write?' I said I thought I did. He said, 'We're going to find out.' He said if I could write, then I could learn about sports." In short order, the high school sophomore was assigned to report on basketball games and bowling tournaments. Later, when reviewing these articles, Gould, the experienced newsman, taught Stephen the art of rewriting. (The news veteran explained, "When you write a story, you're telling yourself the story. When you rewrite, your main job is taking out all the things that are *not* the story.") The process was a revelation for the young man and helped him greatly to refine his writing skills.

Turning Professional Writer

Meanwhile, Stephen continued his fiction writing. Back in 1960, he and friend Chris Chesley had self-published (using the name Triad Publishing Company) *People, Places, and Things—Volume 1*. This 18-page book contained several short stories written by the two young authors. From Stephen's fertile imagination came such entries as "Hotel at the End of the Road," "The Dimension Warp," and "The Thing at the Bottom of the Well." The two young men collaborated on the brief tale "Never Look Behind You." The slim publication contained a foreword, stating that this was "a book for people who would enjoy being pleasantly thrilled for a few moments." It warned, "If you have no imagination, stop right here. This book is not for you." With less than 18 copies published of the first edition, *People, Places, and Things—Volume 1* would become a rare collectors' item in the years ahead.

After several years of unsuccessfully submitting his stories to professional magazines, King finally found acceptance from the fan publication *Comics Review*. In 1965 it published his "I Was a Teenage Grave Robber." His payment was a number of free copies of the issue. Encouraged by this success, Stephen wrote more stories. They often featured people and incidents from his daily life, frequently involving a group of young people caught in unique circumstances. When it came time to eliminate persons in his story line, Stephen would always have the characters he based on his best friends die in a magnificent manner.

Meanwhile, as he continued through Lisbon Falls High, reserved but friendly Stephen became increasingly involved with extracurricular activities. He played on the school's football team (as left tackle). Having taught himself to play rhythm guitar, he formed a rock band (the Mune Spinners) hired to perform at his senior prom.

Also in this period, King turned out his first major work of fiction, *The Aftermath*. The 50,000-word unpublished novel deals with life in the United States after an atomic explosion, reflecting America's continued focus on its Cold War against Russia. In years to come, King would say of such early fiction as *The Aftermath*: "They don't call that stuff 'juvenilia' for nothing. . . . There comes a day when you say to yourself, Good God! If I was this bad, how did I ever get any better?"

The College Years

In the spring of 1966, King graduated from high school. His mother was a great believer in higher education and there was no question that he would go on to college, as his older brother already had. Stephen was offered a partial scholarship to Drew University in Madison, New Jersey. But he could not afford the remaining costs that such enrollment would require. Instead, that fall, he matriculated at the University of Maine at Orono, where his brother was already attending. To pay for incidentals, the King brothers—who both had scholarships—worked part-time jobs. To help them with their expenses, hard-working Mrs. King sent each son $5 weekly. It was only years later, after she had passed away, that Stephen learned that his self-sacrificing mother had often "gone without meals to send that money we'd so casually accepted. It was very unsettling."

As a newcomer to campus life, Stephen felt grossly out of place. Early in his freshman year, as he sat in his dorm room, he noted, "Outside on the grass by Gannett and Androscoggin Hall there were more people playing football than there were in my home town. My few belongings looked pitifully un-collegiate. The room looked mass-produced. I was quite sure my roommate would turn out to be some kind of a freako, or even worse, hopelessly more 'with it' than I."

Like all first-year students, King took basic English composition courses. While he appreciated the intent of such classes and the required writing exercises, he found that such courses "constipated" him. He was also surprised by the rigorous standards of the instructors. (In fact, Stephen received a failing grade on his initial college composition assignment.) To King's benefit, his freshman English instructor, Jim Bishop, took an interest in him and encouraged the fledgling writer to further develop his prose style.

Some years later, by which time Stephen had become a celebrated author, Bishop would recall of his star pupil: "Steve was a nice kid, a good student, but never had a lot of social confidence. Even then, though, he saw himself as a famous writer and thought he could make money at it. Steve was writing continuously, industriously, and diligently. He was amiable, resilient, and created his own world."

King was much happier—and felt more confident— when he was working alone on his own writing, relying on his rapidly developing sense of what was a good story. At the same time, he was disappointed that the American literature courses offered on campus were geared toward studying the classics and assumed that most popular— and contemporary—literature was *not* worth consideration in the curriculum. On the other hand, college gave King a solid foundation in the great pioneers of American prose and poetry, and he started composing verse, a form of creative expression he continued in later years.

In his spare time, King wrote another novel. He was inspired by a rash of campus-based walkathons that raised money for charitable causes. It inspired him to consider what would happen if the concept were taken to a drastic level, in which 100 young men start out on a walk and, by the finish, only one is left alive. The offbeat premise allowed the maturing author to expand his favorite device of psychological horror. When Stephen completed the ambitious manuscript (entitled *The Long Walk*), he showed it to several English professors on campus. They responded with enthusiasm and Stephen optimistically submitted it to a first-novel competition. However, he eventually received a rejection slip. Disappointed but not discouraged, he put the manuscript away, for the time being, in his growing pile of unpublished works.

Diligently pursuing his art and undeterred by his many failures along the way, Stephen kept writing and submitting stories to publications. To his pleasant surprise, in the fall of his sophomore year in college, *Startling Mystery Stories* bought his entry "The Glass Floor" for $35. Looking back to this early professional success, King says, "I've cashed many bigger [checks] since then, but none gave me more satisfaction; someone had finally paid me some real money for something I had found in my head." The next year he would have another story

("Reaper's Image") bought by and published in the same magazine.

Meanwhile, Stephen found an outlet for his writing in the campus literary publication, *Ubris*. One of his entries was "Cain Rose Up." It deals with a student who cracks under the pressure of contemporary life and begins shooting at people from his dorm-room window. The plot concept is based on the notorious incident of Charles Whitman, a University of Texas student, who launched a sniper attack from atop a building tower on that college's campus. Stephen's unusual story—which drew quite a bit of attention from King's classmates— reflects his concerns with the anxieties of life in the 1960s and how the emotional burdens of everyday existence can generate such horrors.

Readjusting His Points of View

When King first entered college, he had been relatively conservative in his political outlook, favoring the Republican Party and Richard M. Nixon (for whom Stephen voted in the 1968 presidential election). However, over subsequent semesters at the university, the fast-maturing King became far more liberal, partly stemming from his growing disgust with America's participation in the Vietnam War. This led him to become involved in civil-rights causes on campus. With his wild mane of long hair and unruly beard, the Maine native looked every bit the radical figure.

To express his political beliefs, Stephen began a column called "King's Garbage Truck," which appeared regularly in the *Maine Campus*, the student newspaper. He wrote on a variety of subjects, always with an impassioned tone that grabbed people's attention. However, his work methodology confounded many on the publication. As a fellow staffer detailed, "King was always late. We would be pulling our hair out at deadline. With five minutes or so to go, Steve would come in and sit down at the typewriter and produce two flawless pages of copy. He carried stories in his head the way most people carry change in their pockets."

Among prolific King's other literary output during his college years was *The Accident*. This one-act play won a university drama award. Another of his writings was "The Gunslinger," which mingled the Old Wild West with sci-fi time travel. One weekend when he was home from college, Stephen showed this work in progress to his friend, Chris Chesley. Intrigued by the story, Chesley had only read a few pages when he enthusiastically voiced, "My god, this is incredible!" Through subsequent years, Chris nagged his buddy to publish this fiction, which eventually became 1984's *The Dark Tower: The Gunslinger*, the start of a multibook saga.

When not writing, Stephen sometimes hung out at a local coffee shop. Since anyone who wished could perform there for the patrons, Stephen took to bringing along his guitar to accompany himself as he sang country-western songs for the crowd. Stephen typically sang downbeat songs of individuals troubled with a rash of bad luck on top of life's ordinary burdens. Many of the listeners rightly assumed that these lyrics reflected the singer's own state of being at the time.

Frequently, King became agitated at school about some new cause. One cause that he took very personally was the lack of academic interest on campus in contemporary popular culture. With the support of two of his favorite professors, King crusaded for an innovative course to be offered at the university on popular literature and culture. King persisted in his belief to the extent that the college administration finally broke with tradition. They eventually allowed him to teach (with the nominal supervision of a full professor) such a campus class. It was the first time an undergraduate had been allowed to do so at this educational institution. Being in charge of the classroom taught Stephen, an English major, that he enjoyed teaching others.

Being practical about his future, Stephen realized that his life as a writer would likely be a tough financial struggle and that he needed a vocation to fall back upon. He worked to gain a teaching certificate. This led him in his senior year of college to student teach at Hampden Academy, located south of Bangor, Maine. After the liberal atmosphere at the university, he was rudely shocked to discover that at the Academy staunch anti-Vietnam War liberals with long hair—such as Stephen—were frowned upon. When he began his student teaching at Hampden, he was forced to cut his hair. Although he reluctantly complied, he angrily wrote about this example of conformity in one of his columns for the university newspaper.

Finding True Love

As obsessed as King was with writing fiction and following through on his heartfelt social and political beliefs, he suddenly found himself involved in a college romance. Among his many part-time jobs (e.g., laundry presser and dishwasher) as a student, he worked at the university's library. There he met another student staff member: Tabitha Jane Spruce, a history major from Old Town, Maine. The third of eight children from a working-class family, she had been forced to abandon her hopes of studying archaeology and history at the University of New Mexico because she could not afford the tuition. Among

Stephen and Tabitha (Corbis)

the many things the two shared in common, King discovered Tabitha had a great love of literature and aspired to be a writer. Before long, the two had fallen in love.

4

ON THE ROAD
TO SUCCESS

On June 5, 1970, Stephen King graduated from the University of Maine at Orono, receiving his B.A. in English and a secondary education teaching certificate. At the time, most young American men who were not (or no longer) in college were being drafted to serve in the military and fight the war in Vietnam. Because of his poor vision and flat feet, King was not one of those called to duty.

Stephen rented a small cabin by the river in Orono so he could be near his girlfriend, Tabitha Spruce, who had one more year to complete her studies at the University. Because teaching positions were scarce, King took whatever work he could find. He accepted a job pumping gas at a local station, earning $1.25 an hour. He improved his lot (moving up to $1.60 an hour) when he accepted another job, working at the New Franklin Laundry in Bangor.

(King's experience at the industrial laundry plant inspired him to write "The Mangler," which was published in his collection of short stories entitled *Night Shift* [1978].)

A Married Man

Years later, King would insist, "The only important thing I ever did in my life for a conscious reason was to ask Tabitha Spruce . . . if she would marry me." The couple married on January 2, 1971 in Old Town, Maine, where Tabitha had grown up. The ceremony was a Catholic service (because Tabitha had been raised in that religion), and the reception was held at a Methodist church (because of Stephen's spiritual upbringing). For the occasion, King borrowed a suit from a friend.

In June 1971, Tabitha graduated from college. Like Stephen, she found it difficult to obtain a decent job and, finally, settled for waitressing at a Dunkin' Donuts in Bangor. With their meager incomes, the couple barely squeaked by. Stephen sold the occasional story to a magazine, but the money always came at just the moment they had some insurmountable bill to pay.

Hampden Academy offered Stephen a full-time teaching post with an annual salary of $6,400. He was assigned to teach basic literature and creative writing courses to the high school students. King jumped at the opportunity. In September 1971, he began his full schedule at Hampden Academy. He proved an apt instructor in the classroom. One of his students would say years later, "He was a good teacher who had seven classes a day and a study hall. He told us that he liked to write, and I think he wanted us to write. He was fun and had a pretty good sense of humor."

Although teaching—and all the course preparation and paper grading that went with it—was a constantly demanding task, King never abandoned his freelance writing. Every free minute he had during the day, he would find a quiet place at school (usually in the building's boiler room) to jot down several paragraphs or even a few sentences of his latest story. Robert W. Rowe, principal at Hampden Academy, later recalled of Stephen: "If he had the spare time, he'd be reading a book. But he always took the time to write. He was disciplined in his writing, consistent in sitting down and doing the work."

Each evening when King returned home to the modest double-wide trailer he and Tabitha shared, he did not let his exhaustion from the long work hours prevent his ritual of writing for about two hours before he went to bed. He would sit scrunched up in a corner of the trailer, using an old child's desktop as a writing surface, all the time feeling guilty for stealing time from other obligations. With this continued output of fiction, King was more frequently selling his stories to national magazines.

If King's extended work day was not demanding enough month in and month out, there were always the financial pressures of supporting his growing household. In 1971, Tabitha gave birth to their first child, Naomi, and, in 1972, to Joseph. In addition, Stephen sent his mother money on a monthly basis; she had developed cancer and could no longer work. To help pay their ever-increasing bills, the Kings let Stephen's boyhood pal, Chris Chesley (who was completing college), rent a room in their cramped environment. Even with this added income, the financially hard-pressed Kings had to bypass necessary repairs on their old car or, for months at a time, have their phone turned off.

Even with his growing responsibilities as a father and husband, Stephen never abandoned writing. (Photofest)

As this wearing lifestyle continued—which included returning to work at the laundry plant during the summer break from Hampden Academy—King became engulfed in self-doubts. While doing his best to hide his negative moods from everyone, he turned increasingly to drinking beer and liquor and to using stimulants to mask his fears and exhaustion. These habits would become a source of many difficulties in King's personal and creative life in later years.

While he enjoyed teaching and found great satisfaction in writing, the constant financial burdens ate away at Stephen's self-confidence. Having two babies who needed medical attention, as all infants do, put the family further into debt. Stephen also felt great remorse that Tabitha was taking on most of the responsibilities of caring for the infants and keeping the modest household going. The depressing situation reached a point where, as King recalled, "I began to have long talks with myself at night about whether or not I was chasing a fool's dreams." He became progressively angry and frustrated with life and found it increasingly difficult to keep his dour feelings bottled up. He coped with the gnawing aggravation by drinking and smoking to excess and playing weekly card games for money—none of which the tightly budgeted family could afford.

Making a Career Decision

Selling an occasional story to a magazine for $200 to $300 certainly was a help to King's financial situation. Stephen realized, however, that if he was to succeed as a full-time author and earn a livable wage from his craft, he must devote himself to creating novels. In his spare time, he wrote *Getting It On*. It tells of a rebellious young student who is expelled from high school for menacing a teacher. Later, he returns to the classroom, kills the instructor, and holds his terrified classmates hostage. Meanwhile, law enforcers surround the building, leading to a deadly climax.

Always an avid reader, Stephen had read and enjoyed *The Parallax View*, by Loren Singer, which Doubleday and Co. had published in 1970. King felt there were parallels in the style of that novel and *Getting It On*. He shipped his manuscript to this New York-based major publishing firm. He addressed his package to the attention of the editor of *The Parallax View*, not knowing that the individual had already left the publishing house. Because Stephen's manuscript arrived at Doubleday unsolicited and not pre-sented by a known literary agent, it was placed on the *slush pile*, unsolicited manuscripts that any in-house edi-tor can browse through and pursue, if interested. Eventu-ally, seasoned editor Bill Thompson came across King's manuscript.

After reading *Getting It On*, Thompson contacted Stephen and stated that while he found the novel inter-esting, it required revisions. King eagerly agreed to make the suggested changes. Some time later, the editor informed Stephen that although he believed in the revamped work, unfortunately, Doubleday's editorial board had vetoed acquiring the novel. The rejection was a huge blow to the author "because I had been allowed to entertain some hope for an extraordinarily long time and had rewritten the book a third time, trying to bring it into line with what Doubleday's publishing board would accept."

Believing King to be a writer of great promise, Thompson stayed in touch with Stephen, encouraging him to submit more fiction to Doubleday. The editor's continued faith did a great deal to boost Stephen's sagging morale amidst his financial woes and pressing family duties. Decades later, King would say of Thompson: "He was that all-important first contact that new writers wait and wish for . . . and so seldom find."

With Thompson's ongoing support, King turned out two additional novels (*Babylon Here* and *Sword of Darkness*), which he shipped to Doubleday. Both of these manuscripts were also turned down. The repeated rejections were crushing to Stephen, but he persisted with his vision that he was a constantly improving writer worthy of major publication. Philosophically, he told himself that these declined fictions were part of his paying his dues in the writing profession.

A Reward for Patience

During 1972, between his teaching and household obligations, King began a new book. His inspiration came from a female coworker whom he had observed a few years earlier at the laundry plant where he had worked. The woman was deeply religious and often spouted off quotes from the Bible. At the time, Stephen had wondered what this individual was like on the home front and how her behavior affected her children. This premise had been percolating in King's mind for some time. Now ready to write the story, he utilized two female outsiders he had met as inspiration for the woman character's daughter: One of the females was a current student at Hampden Academy; the other was a former high school classmate of his. What gave the developing plot a special Kingsian twist was that the teenage heroine, harassed by her bizarre mother and her insensitive classmates, has special telekinetic powers (including the ability to set objects on fire).

Stephen wrote four or five pages of the narrative before he became discouraged with his efforts. He was convinced that the key figures (both women) were not believable females because, in essence, he felt he hardly understood the opposite sex. Annoyed with his short draft, he tossed the pages into the trash. Shortly thereafter, while doing housecleaning chores, Tabitha noticed the pages in the rubbish, retrieved them, and read the text. A budding writer herself, she was impressed with what her husband had written. She convinced him to continue with this tale. Because he respected his wife's evaluation, he agreed.

By January 1973, King had completed the book, titled *Carrie* after the name of the daughter character, and shipped it off to Bill Thompson at Doubleday. The editor was impressed with his protégée's latest effort, but suggested ways to improve it. Stephen willingly made the required changes, including lengthening the story so it would qualify as a novella (a short novel). After reading the new version, Thompson invited Stephen to Doubleday's offices in New York to discuss the book. Borrowing $75 from his wife's grandmother, King took the bus to Manhattan. Arriving in town several hours before the scheduled meeting, he walked about the city, which he had never visited before, and gawked at the skyscrapers.

By the time he reached Thompson's office, his feet were blistered from the new shoes he had bought for the occasion and he was exhausted. At lunch he had two drinks. Because he had not eaten in a while, he became a bit drunk. He felt he really messed up his chances with Thompson when he ordered a pasta dish and bits of the fettuccini stuck in his heavy beard as he consumed the food. Throughout the meeting, the editor remained understanding of the author's nervousness and clumsiness, insisting that *Carrie* had a real good chance of being accepted by the Doubleday board.

King returned to Maine, convinced he had made a bad impression at the luncheon and that *Carrie* would probably meet the same fate as his past submissions. He went about his usual routine of teaching and writing. Then, one day while Stephen was at school, a communication from Bill Thompson came to the Kings' trailer. (Because the author's phone had been turned off that month, the editor had sent a telegram.) After reading it, an excited Tabitha rushed to a neighbor's to use the phone. She called her husband at Hampden Academy and read him the message: "CARRIE OFFICIALLY A DOUBLEDAY BOOK. $2,500 ADVANCE AGAINST ROYALTIES. CONGRATS KID—THE FUTURE LIES AHEAD."

When Stephen came home that afternoon, Tabitha waved the telegram at him and the two embraced, jumped around, and cried with joy.

Tasting Success

King's advance of $2,500 on *Carrie* was a decent amount in 1973, especially for a first-time novelist. (Once the publisher had earned back the cost of the advance from book sales, Stephen would receive royalties—a percentage of the book sales—on his novel.) With the advance, the Kings not only took care of many overdue bills, but bought a replacement car, a blue Ford Pinto, and moved from the trailer to an apartment in a working-class section of Bangor.

With his career moving into professional status, King could not wait for *Carrie*'s publication, which was scheduled for April 5, 1974. Having committed to the book, Doubleday was now publicizing it heavily. Tapping into the horror readership market that had made such earlier books as *Rosemary's Baby* and *The Exorcist* big hits (both turned into extremely successful Hollywood movies), the publisher promoted their upcoming release as "*the* novel of the year."

Doubleday printed 30,000 hardback copies of *Carrie*. The book received mixed to good reviews. *Library Journal* considered it "an interesting idea, but none of the characters is really very believable and the final orgy of destruction is terribly overdone." In contrast, the *New York Times* judged that the bloody story was "one guaranteed to give you a chill. . . . that this is a first novel is amazing." The book sold a respectable 13,000 copies in hardback. Overall, Stephen was pleased by the response, but saddened that his mother, who had died of cancer in December 1973, did not live to see his emergence into the book world.

Meanwhile, Doubleday's subsidiary rights department had undertaken the next step, selling the paperback rights to *Carrie*. To the publishing house's amazement, they received an offer from New American Library for a whopping $400,000. If Doubleday was flabbergasted by the huge sale, King was ecstatic to learn that he would be receiving $200,000, his contractual half-share of the negotiations.

With this huge windfall and now able to become a full-time writer, Stephen reluctantly ended his teaching career at Hampden Academy, where he had so enjoyed his time with the students. As he explained, he could now "fulfill what I believe is my only function in life: to write books. Good, bad, or indifferent books, that's for others to decide; it's enough to write."

Astounded by their sudden financial salvation, Stephen couldn't wait to buy his patient, supportive wife a gift of appreciation. Anxious to make a purchase, he rushed to a nearby store and bought the first thing he saw that he thought Tabitha would like and could use: a $16 electric hair dryer.

When the mass-market paperback of *Carrie* reached the book racks around the country in 1975, it soon sold over 1 million copies. But what really sold the paperback (and more copies of the hardback edition) was the October 1976 release of a film version of *Carrie*. Directed by Brian De Palma and adapted to the screen by Lawrence D. Cohen, the chiller starred Sissy Spacek in the title role, Piper Laurie as her mother, and included in its cast the up-and-coming John Travolta. Made for a relatively modest $1.8 million, the picture earned strong reviews and went on to enjoy domestic theater rentals of $12.5 million. For their performances in this well-regarded feature, both Spacek and Laurie were Oscar-nominated.

Sissy Spacek in Carrie *(1976)* (Photofest)

As a result of the box-office success of *Carrie*, there was a great public demand to read the book, and the paperback edition went on to sell over a total of 3.5 million copies. It was a rare instance of a movie tie-in to a book leading to such an astounding success. Because of the film's popularity—and renewed interest in the book version of *Carrie*—Stephen King was suddenly a name to reckon with in the publishing industry. The author observed, "The movie made the book and the book made me." (*Carrie,* having been a 1988 Broadway musical

and remade for TV in 2002, had a film sequel in 1999—
The Rage:Carrie 2.)

Not one to rest on his laurels, during this period after
the book sale of _Carrie_, King had kept busy at his craft. (As
he later admitted, by this time he was also becoming
involved increasingly in substance abuse.) His next literary venture was based on his pondering what would happen if Dracula, the memorable vampire character from
Bram Stoker's literary classic, should suddenly appear in
present-day Maine. This intriguing conjecture led Stephen
to write his next novel—one destined to greatly further his
writing reputation.

5

THE BEST-SELLING AUTHOR

In the summer of 1973, the King family rented a home in North Windham, Maine, a small community near Sebago Lake, not far from Durham. In this relaxed atmosphere, Stephen worked on *The Second Coming*. It is a hair-raising account of a successful author returning to his sleepy home town of Jerusalem Lot in Maine to write his new book. He soon discovers that vampires have infested this New England village to prey on its unsuspecting inhabitants. This gruesome premise sets into motion what would become a familiar King theme—the battle between good and evil forces told amidst heavy dashes of chilling horror and gripping plot turns. (The novel was inspired by the story "Jerusalem's Lot" that King wrote in

1967 for a college course, a tale that would be published in Stephen's 1978 story collection *Night Shift*.)

As with *Carrie*, King followed the advice of his editor and drastically revised the sprawling story. When finally accepted, the manuscript was retitled *'Salem's Lot*. It was scheduled for publication in 1975. Again, New American Library bought the paperback rights to the book, this time paying $500,000.

Developing a Writing Schedule

Freed from the burden of an outside job to support his family, Stephen had established a writing routine he would follow strictly for many years to come. In the mornings, after a long walk, he wrote for approximately three hours on his current project. In the afternoon, besides attending to business matters and correspondence, he typically devoted a few hours to jotting down ideas for a forthcoming book project. In addition, he devoted several hours during the day to reading works of new and old favorite authors. He followed this demanding practice every day of the week all year long, rarely breaking his schedule even on his birthday or Christmas.

Part of Stephen's compulsive work habits can be traced to his earnest mother, who constantly fretted about being prepared for life's unexpected obstacles. She worked hard to have resources at hand to meet any potential emergency.

Very early in his career, Stephen developed a strict writing routine that he still follows today. (Photofest)

With his strong work ethic, King was able to turn out six pages of manuscript a day, an average of 2,000 words. For him, being a writer was a serious job that demanded diligence and a structured schedule.

When creating a novel, King typically put the manuscript through three, or even four, drafts. In his viewpoint, in the first go-round, "most of what you want should be there." This included having a cast of realistic characters with whom the reader could become involved. According to King, "The second draft is especially critical." He explained that often it was not until the initial version was completed that the author had a clear vision of the whole book. This sudden understanding of the full story he likened to "drawing pictures in a dark room, and then a sudden illumination shows you what you've been drawing. Before you write it down, the story exists, but it takes the actual writing to recognize it." Therefore, King's approach to writing often required revamping the earlier part of the novel. "On the third draft," King said, "I concentrate on language and make the sentences feel balanced. Good writing should be accessible."

Reviewers of *'Salem's Lot* noted several key influences in King's Gothic suspense tale. These ranged from Bram Stoker's *Dracula* (1897) to the stories of 19th-century New England writer Nathaniel Hawthorne, who wrote of morality, sin, and guilt. Some observers found parallels in

Stephen's book to the harsh aspects of small-town life as depicted in Grace Metalious's best-seller *Peyton Place* (1956).

In interviews, Stephen mentioned that he gained further inspiration for *'Salem's Lot* from the EC horror comics he had read as a kid, as well as from several of his favorite horror/science-fiction movies, especially *Invasion of the Body Snatchers* (1956). King also observed that, like other horror writers, he felt himself obliged to be a source of calming the "fears and anxieties and insecurities" so prevalent in our complex contemporary life. Spelling out such author tasks, he said that horror writers are ". . . sitting in the darkness beyond the flickering warmth of your fire, cackling into our cauldrons and spinning out our spider webs of words, all the time sucking the sickness from your minds and spewing it out into the night."

Like *Carrie*, *'Salem's Lot* would be sold to the movies, but, again, with no provision for Stephen to write the screenplay. No one seemed to be able to condense the 405-page novel into a workable film, so the property was resold to a TV producer to be made as a two-part miniseries. Although King was concerned that presenting his story on television would cause artistic problems (e.g., distracting breaks in the story to permit commercials and having to censor some of the violence and gore for TV audiences), he appreciated that the miniseries format would permit much more of his tale to be presented on screen. The TV miniseries *'Salems Lot* aired in November 1979, and King was generally pleased with the adaptation of his novel.

A Shining Success

Thanks to the paperback sale of *Carrie* in May 1974, money was no longer an issue in the King household. Now Stephen felt a strong need for a change of scenery, and since his children were not yet of school age, there was no concern about uprooting them from the classroom. He wasn't sure where the family should relocate, however. Tabitha suggested they open up a map of the United States. Next, she blindfolded Stephen and told him to put his finger on the atlas. It led them to moving to Boulder, Colorado in the late summer of 1974.

That fall, King spent several weeks working on a novel called *The House on Value Street*, based, to a degree, on the kidnapping and brainwashing of newspaper heiress Patty Hearst. When the story would not come together, he wisely put it aside. He next tried a premise involving a psychic boy who, with his family, was cut off from the outside world at an amusement park. Once again, he experienced writer's block in which his ideas would not solidify into a usable plot line with good character development. About such occupational hazards he later said, "When I can't work, I tell myself it will pass. I am compulsive. If I don't write, a voice inside agitates for the work. If you don't use it, you'll lose it. I've had periods when I've written nothing but crap for as long as a year."

To help clear his mind, Stephen suggested that he and Tabitha take a brief vacation. They had heard of the Stanley Hotel, a famous old resort about 45 miles northwest of Boulder and went there for a weekend. When they arrived, the hotel was about to close for the winter and they were the only guests. As King roamed the long, dark hotel corridors, walked about his old-fashioned oversized bathroom, and ate with his wife in the huge dining room (in which they were the only patrons), a bizarre story began to gel in his fertile mind.

When the couple returned to Boulder, Stephen rented an office in the downtown area so he could have peace and quiet to write his new project. Borrowing the character of the boy with telekinetic powers from his recent unfinished project, he quickly spun out a new novel called *The Shining.* As always, the latest work had many biographical elements. The story revolved around a former teacher who is alcoholic (something Stephen knew all too much about) who makes one final stab at being the backbone of his family. He takes a job as the winter caretaker of the Overlook Hotel in the Colorado Rocky Mountains. His wife, his son, and he are the only inhabitants of this isolated resort. Before long, the man's distressing past and his troubled present life catch up with him, midst the many demon spirits emerging from the spooky hotel. The chilling tale combines story elements of a marriage falling apart, a man descending into madness, and a murderous rampage, as well as an innocent boy with a special power (the Shining) to peer into the future.

One of King's strong literary influences in writing *The Shining* was Shirley Jackson's classic novel, *The Haunting of Hill House* (1959), which Stephen regards as a great genre piece. Twenty-seven-year-old Stephen completed the first draft of *The Shining* in less than four months. After the necessary revisions, 50,000 copies of *The Shining* were published in early 1977. As before, King's new offering became an even bigger hit in its paperback edition, selling a combined total of over 2 million copies. An author whose latest book had made the *New York Times* best-seller list, Stephen was fast becoming America's leading horror writer.

Esteemed filmmaker Stanley Kubrick purchased the screen rights to *The Shining*. He passed on using Stephen's submitted screenplay for the project, preferring to collaborate with Diane Johnson on his own vision. Made for $19 million, the elaborate 1980 feature was a box-office hit, grossing nearly $40 million in domestic distribution. However, it received mixed reviews and was publicly criticized by King as pretentious and an ineffectual thriller. In a 1982 *TV Guide* interview, King termed Kubrick's loose film adaptation "cold and disappointingly loveless." Stephen eventually had the opportunity to right the artistic wrong. In 1997, he provided the teleplay for a TV miniseries version of *The Shining*.

Creating a Pseudonym—Richard Bachman

By 1975, the Kings had moved back to Maine. They bought a ranch house sitting on 2.65 acres in Bridgton, a small town some 40 miles northwest of Portland. Also that year, the University of Maine at Orono established an archive of Stephen's writing. In this period, Stephen became politically active again, joining in successful opposition to censorship of books in his home state. As an author whose own volumes would often be banned in various parts of the country due to their violent and gory sequences, Stephen felt strongly on the issue and has remained always an active supporter of freedom of the written word.

In 1977, the year in which the Kings became parents of son Owen, a novel called *Rage* was published. Authored by Richard Bachman, the paperback original passed relatively unknown in the marketplace, selling only around 22,000 copies. Actually, Stephen authored the book, which centers on a vengeful student holding a high-school class

Stephen speaks to a crowd at his alma mater, the University of Maine at Orono, which houses an archive of his writing. (Associated Press)

hostage. He completed it during his college years. King created the pseudonym Richard Bachman to bypass the publishing industry's traditional rule that a well-known writer should not publish more than one book each year. This concept was too restricting for an author of King's prolific nature. Using a pen name or pseudonym, from Stephen's point of view, also gave him the freedom of not having to meet the public's high expectations of a new Stephen King novel.

For a few years, King would be able to keep the alias pretty much a secret. Continuing with the use of his Richard Bachman pseudonym, Stephen's *The Long Walk*, another novel from his college days, was published in 1979. It made little stir in the publishing world, nor did *Roadwork* (1981) or *The Running Man* (1982), two later Bachman entries.

In 1984, *Thinner*, the fifth Richard Bachman-authored novel, was published. By this point, several reviewers and many King enthusiasts suspected that Bachman was actually King. This was confirmed when Steve Brown, a Washington, D.C., bookshop clerk, visited the Library of Congress and examined the copyright registrations for each Bachman work. He discovered that on *Rage*, a publishing-house employee had accidentally listed King as the author of that book, rather than Bachman, which was a registered pen name. Because the author never saw these forms before they were filed, King never caught the error.

Then, in January 1985, Brown informed King of his intriguing discovery. A few weeks later, the TV tabloid show *Entertainment Tonight* hinted at the connection between King and Bachman. Next, in the second issue of *Castle Rock*, the Stephen King newsletter which ran from 1985 to 1989, it was announced that a "secret [would be] revealed at last" in an upcoming issue. Before this occurred, a *Bangor Daily News* reporter wrote an article for the newspaper's February 9, 1985 issue, entitled "Pseudonym Kept Five King Novels a Mystery." The secret was out. This led to the republication of the first four Bachman novels along with the piece "Why I Was Bachman." As for *Thinner*, which had sold only modestly under the Bachman name, it now went into three additional, huge printings.

Living Abroad—Briefly

Meanwhile in 1977, Stephen relocated his family to England. He planned to stay there a year to write a ghost story. Before embarking on the grand adventure, he put an ad in British newspapers that read, "Wanted, a draughty Victorian house in the country with dark attic and creaking floorboards, preferably haunted." It led to the Kings renting a large house in Fleet, Hampshire. Not only did the new address prove *not* to be haunted, but Stephen could not get his new literary project to take shape. Instead, another plot idea began to evolve in his mind. He had recently read in a Portland, Maine, newspaper about a rabid St. Bernard dog that attacked and killed a young boy. This tragic mishap set King to thinking about his own experience with a menacing St. Bernard when he had taken his motorcycle to a local Maine garage for repairs. It led the author to start work on the novel *Cujo*.

During this British period, Stephen began a friendship with American horror writer Peter Straub (author of *Ghost Story*), who was living nearby with his wife. Years later, in 1984, King collaborated with Straub on the novel *The Talisman* and again, in 2001, on *Black House*.

Continued Success

In late 1977, having drafted an initial full version of *Cujo*, the Kings left England. They had remained abroad for only three months. They now purchased a new Maine home in Center Lovell, a quaint town on Kezar Lake near the New Hampshire border. In 1978, Doubleday published *Night Shift*, a collection of King's short stories. Later in the year came *The Stand*. At 823 pages, it was an extremely lengthy novel, but the original manuscript had actually been 400 pages longer. However, much to King's anger, the publisher demanded severe cuts to save on production costs.

The mammoth narrative—a mixture of science fiction, horror, and fantasy—was based on an actual mid-1970s accidental spill of a chemical-biological weapon in Utah that could easily have turned into a huge disaster. Stephen's tale focuses on a horrendous man-made plague (known as Captain Trips) set loose, in error, by the military. The plague nearly destroys all life on Earth. The survivors divide into two opposing forces: The good are led by an elderly woman named Mother Abigail, while the evil camp is guided by a demonic man named Randall Flagg. The ultimate showdown between the two groups occurs around Las Vegas. Even in its edited-down version, the work became a major hit and remains one of readers' favorite writings by King.

In 1990, Doubleday issued a new edition of *The Stand*, this time restoring 150,000 words of King's original text. In the expanded version, for which the author wrote a special two-part preface, the story line is updated to the present day, and there are several new characters in the plot. In 1994, the TV miniseries *The Stand* appeared on ABC.

Having hardly settled into their new residence, the Kings moved yet again in 1978. The University of Maine at Orono inaugurated a program that brought well-known authors on campus to be writers/teachers in residence. Under the prompting of his past professor Burton Hatlen, Stephen agreed to teach four classes—two literature courses, and one each in creative writing and poetry—during the 1978–1979 academic year. The King family rented a two-story house in Orrington.

Their new home was on Route 15, a main thoroughfare for trucks speeding to and from nearby Bangor. On this windy, hilly terrain, few of the big rigs ever braked for any little animal that scurried across its path. As a result, several cats, dogs, and other animals—often household pets—

Stephen on the set of the TV miniseries The Stand *(1994)*
(Photofest)

had been killed on the busy road. The neighborhood children had a custom of burying such traffic victims in a special hillside area that boasted a sign reading "Pet Sematary" (using the youngsters' phonetic spelling of the word).

On Thanksgiving 1979, the Kings' first-born, Naomi, lost her beloved cat Smucky on this roadway. It was as traumatic for the parents to tell their girl of the sad event as it was for the grieving child. From this distressing episode sprang an idea that, in addition to inspiration from W. W. Jacobs's story "The Monkey's Paw," led Stephen to write the novel *Pet Sematary*. The depressing tale tells of the death and return to life of a beloved family cat and, later, a deceased child. According to King, because the account is so bleak, "The book ceased being a novel to me, and became instead a gloomy exercise, like an endless marathon run. It never left my mind, it never ceased to trouble me." King was so downhearted by his frightening story that he put it away in a drawer to be revised—and then published—at some future date.

Not until 1983 was *Pet Sematary* finally published; it emerged under strange circumstances. King had grown increasingly dissatisfied with his contractual arrangement and treatment at Doubleday, his New York-based publishing house. In particular, there was a clause in his book contracts that allowed him to receive only $50,000 a year from royalties on past Doubleday-published Stephen King books. Because of Stephen's hefty book sales, it would take many decades for King to be paid all that he was owed. To retrieve these sizeable reserve funds—and to remain safely within Internal Revenue Service guidelines—King had to offer the publisher a final novel in exchange. This turned out to be *Pet Sematary*. The book was a best-seller. Six years later, it became a film, the first movie made from one of his works to actually utilize Stephen's own screenplay. (In addition, King had a cameo in the movie, playing a minister. It was the first of several such bit parts he would have in features made from his writings.) Although most critics heartily disliked the picture, it was, nevertheless, a financial hit.

Meanwhile, having fulfilled his contractual obligations to Doubleday, Stephen found a new publisher. Kirby McCauley, a literary agent who specialized in King's literary genres and who had become friendly with the author in recent times, negotiated a new lucrative $2.5 million pact for Stephen with New American Library. Thus, as of 1979, NAL would continue to print paperback versions of King's offerings, while Viking Press would now publish hardback editions of his latest works.

With this rewarding professional transition, Stephen had graduated to the major leagues in his profession.

6

AT THE TOP OF HIS PROFESSION

In 1979 Stephen King's *The Dead Zone* was published. It involves a young man who, as the result of an accident, finds he has special mental powers that allow him to see into the future. King enthused of his newest entry, "I'm very proud of that book. It says serious things about the political structure of America and how it's set up." (The highly imaginative *Dead Zone* would be adapted to the screen in 1983. In 2002, the book inspired a weekly cable TV series starring Anthony Michael Hall.)

A Magnificent House

Having long sought a permanent winter home, in 1980 the Kings purchased a sprawling 124-year-old Victorian mansion in Bangor, Maine. As a youngster, Tabitha had often passed the impressive old house and dreamed of living there one day. Built in the 1850s, it was an elaborate Italianate villa with 23 rooms and two towers; the house required extensive alterations so that its new owners could use the dwelling both for their home and for their business. The renovations included installing stained-glass bat windows, offices for both Stephen and Tabitha, and an indoor swimming pool. These renovations took four years to complete.

Since they had never been carried away by their new-found notoriety, the Kings hoped that they would not have to fence off their new property. Despite a police-issued "Do Not Disturb" sign posted by the front doorbell, determined fans—of which there were an ever-increasing number—made pilgrimages to Bangor and turned the home into a tourist attraction. These persistent devotees hoped to see King in person, get autographs, and/or take a picture with the famed writer. Eventually, the family was forced to buy 11,000 pounds of hand-forged fencing to section off the house from the public. The fence contained two gates featuring iron work that incorporated shapes of winged bats, spiders, webs, and goat heads. Later, the fencing was extended to encompass the entire property, and the front gates were always locked.

Despite these security measures, the Kings experienced a terrifying incident in 1991. Tabitha was home alone one day when a mentally unbalanced individual broke in through a kitchen window. Confronting Mrs. King, he warned her that he had a homemade bomb and would use it unless his list of demands was met. As quickly as she could, Tabitha fled the house and called the police. When the disturbed man was captured by the police, they discovered that his bomb was a fake. Nevertheless, the scary incident led the Kings to install closed-circuit TV cameras to monitor the property.

America's most popular writer at the gates of his house in Bangor, Maine. (The Image Works)

A Nonfiction Release

Stephen's next book was a departure from his usual work. His one-time Doubleday editor, Bill Thompson, suggested he write a book in which Stephen "could say everything that . . . [he] thought about horror fiction, horror movies, and what it all means." The result was 1981's *Danse Macabre*. The *Baltimore Sun* enthused that the nonfiction entry "succeeds on any number of levels, as pure horror memorabilia for longtime ghoulie groupies, as a bibliography for younger addicts weaned on King and as an insightful noncredit course for would-be writers of the genre." In the introduction, Stephen notes, "It's my Final Statement on the clockwork of the horror tale."

Stephen was not the only King family member to have a book published in 1981. That year Tabitha authored *Small World*, the first of her several novels to date. While her writing never sold to the degree of her husband's, she developed a fine reputation as a sterling regional writer, one whose works reflected a strong sense of humanity.

Tackling the Movies

While several of Stephen King's works had been adapted to the big and small screen, the writer had yet to partici-pate actively in any such film projects. This was remedied in 1982 when moviemaker George A. Romero (*The Night of the Living Dead*) suggested King write an original screenplay. It was to be an anthology of horror tales that would replicate the underlying terror created by such 1950s works as William F. Gaines's EC comic books. Within two months, Stephen had completed his script, which contained five episodes.

Creepshow (1982) was shot on an $8 million budget. King was persuaded to take a sizeable acting role in the project. In the comedic segment, "The Lonesome Death of Jordy Verrill" (which derived from King's 1976 short story "Weeds"), Stephen plays the dim-witted title character, who finds himself altered into an alien mass of green fungus. At first, King enjoyed the daily transformation process that involved six hours of makeup work, but the process soon became a bore. It curbed his desire to tackle future major acting assignments.

Although most critics found *Creepshow* artistically weak, the good-natured and at times gross picture made a profit. To tie in with the picture's release, New American Library issued a paperback novelization of the movie that contains arresting illustrations by Bernie Wrightson.

Reviewers were far less kind to subsequent film adaptations of King's published works. For example, *Christine* (1983) and *Children of the Corn* (1984) were so artistically disappointing that many discerning moviegoers began avoiding screen adaptations of King's works.

When Stephen's novel *Firestarter* (1980) was sold for a screen adaptation, King was convinced that it was a "more 'movie-able' book than some of my others." Unfortunately, the 1984 film was more concerned with its fiery special effects than with its story and characters. Another release the same year was *Cat's Eye,* based on King's original screenplay that utilized three of the author's tales. It was a box-office flop.

In this period, it seemed that no movie adapted from a King work could receive critical plaudits. Often, these ventures made only a small box-office profit, based largely on the drawing power of Stephen's name.

The Prizewinner

In 1980, Stephen had been named *People* magazine's Writer of the Year. In 1982, he was given the Hugo Award for *Danse Macabre*, the British Fantasy Award for *Cujo*, and the World Fantasy Award for "Do the Dead Sing?" a 1981 story that reverts to its original title, "The Reach," when included in King's 1985 popular story collection, *Skeleton Crew*.

Long a car lover, King combined this affection with his strong interest in rock and roll and the problems of teenage anxiety to create *Christine* (1983). In the novel, a teenager's passion for his car—a 1958 Plymouth Fury with a mind of its own—becomes obsessive, leading to a deadly finale. Of this book, King admitted, "I've been very lucky with reviews over the years with the exception of *Christine,* which was just *roasted*!"

When Stephen's 12-year-old daughter read *Cujo* in 1983, she was upset by the frightening book and vowed never to read her dad's works again. To remedy this, King wrote *The Eyes of the Dragon* (1984), a fairy tale. Set in the realm of Delain, the story tells of two brothers pitted against each for control of the crown. The tale also involves the dastardly Randall Flagg, a character from *The Stand.* The delightful narrative not only pleased the writer's children, but any others fortunate enough to acquire one of the few original copies: The initial printing of the book was a deluxe limited edition from Philtrum Press, King's self-publishing venture. Heeding his fans' demands for greater access to this work, King finally allowed Viking to publish a trade edition in 1987.

Taking Another Stab at the Movies

Unhappy with the way his movies were being brought to the screen, King took matters into his own hands. He not only wrote the original screenplay to *Maximum Overdrive* (1986), but directed the film. He wanted to prove his belief that he "could probably make a movie that would scare a lot of people very *badly.*" He also acknowledged, "I *think* I have the capability, but I'm not sure. I might really screw it up." Giving himself ample preproduction time, Stephen, who had no film-school training, went on location in 1985 to direct the feature for producer Dino De Laurentiis. He was paid $70,000 for this first-time effort.

Maximum Overdrive, like his earlier story *Christine*, deals with a vehicle that has a mind of its own—only this time several trucks and other machinery run amuck at a truck stop. The directing experience proved daunting for King, especially because so few of the Italian crew at De Laurentiis's studio spoke English. During the shoot, King learned the hard way how being a director involves grueling work and long hours.

Maximum Overdrive—which cost $10 million to make—was panned by the critics, who lambasted Stephen's directorial abilities. The unsatisfactory movie drew in only $7.43 million in domestic distribution. Later, Stephen acknowledged that he had spent too much time with the technical aspects of the film's special effects and too little attention to characterization and pacing. Asked if he would ever again direct a picture, Stephen responded, "I can't see myself doing anything like this again, at least not until my family has all grown up. I want to be around to enjoy them while I can."

In sharp contrast, 1986 was also the year of a marvelous Stephen King feature film—*Stand By Me*. Based on his novella *The Body*, from his 1982 collection *Different Sea-*

Stephen made his directorial debut with the film Maximum Overdrive *(1986) after being unhappy with several film adaptations of his works.* (Photofest)

sons, the film was directed by Rob Reiner and starred the young actors Wil Wheaton, River Phoenix, Corey Feldman, and Jerry O'Connell. The movie was a nostalgic look at boyhood friendships in the 1950s and was inspired by the boyhood trauma Stephen had suffered when his pal was run over by a freight train. The movie received tremendous reviews and went on to gross millions in domestic distribution. When King saw a screening of the picture, he was so affected by the story—and by all the repressed memories it brought back—that he had to spend several minutes alone to collect his thoughts.

Moving On

In *It* (1986), a complex tale set in the fictional Maine town of Derry and covering three decades and utilizing two time frames, Stephen again focused on monsters and children, bringing together several themes from his past novels. According to King, *It* was "a final summing up of everything I've tried to say in the last twelve years on the two central subjects of my fiction." The 1,142-page book was far from an easy read and had its share of detractors. *Newsweek* complained about the "mechanical showdown and shockeroos" and dismissed the book's "ideas." The *New York Times Book Review* asked, "Where did Stephen King, the most experienced prince of darkness, go wrong with *It*? Almost everywhere." But because Stephen King was practically a brand name at this point, the book was automatically purchased by his legion of readers. In 1990, *It* became an ABC miniseries.

The Tommyknockers (1987) is a book about aliens whose spaceship lands on Earth millions of years ago near what is now Haven, Maine. In the present day, this once-buried UFO and its mysterious passengers, the Tommyknockers, exert a powerful physical and psychological influence over the townsfolk, causing weird repercussions. The narrative reflected King's ongoing concerns with the dangers of nuclear weapons and high technology and the potential of radiation pollution poisoning the Earth. In 1993, this book also became a television miniseries.

King's other 1987 novel was *The Dark Tower II: The Drawing of the Three*, which continued the exciting and offbeat book series begun with 1984's *The Dark Tower: The Gunslinger*. Derived from a work begun in college, the series—projected to include seven volumes—owes much to stories of epic fantasy quest and to the rash of Spaghetti westerns made in Italy in the 1960s and 1970s.

Misery

Having enjoyed tremendous commercial success over the last several years, King was extremely conscious of the tenuous and often difficult relationship between a celebrity and his demanding fans. With his usual imaginative twist, Stephen took the association several macabre steps further in *Misery* (1987). The book's premise owes a bit to John Fowles's *The Collector* (1963), one of King's favorite novels. In harrowing terms, *Misery* tells of a successful romance genre writer who ends the life of his popular heroine, Misery Chastain. Later, after suffering an auto accident, he is cared for by a strange woman named Annie Wilkes, who claims to be his number-one fan. After becoming very upset by the death of Misery, she demands that the author revive the character in a book sequel. Because the writer fears for his life from this demented and violent admirer, he must bend to her every whim to keep alive. Describing the book in an issue of the *Castle Rock* newsletter, Tabitha King pointed out, "*Misery* is not the first novel to examine the relationship between writer and reader, or between celebrity and fan, but its exploration of the worst aspects of the celebrity-fan connection is obvious and real."

Publishers Weekly was among the many reviewing sources to recognize a new maturity in King's writing. Labeling the book "unadulteratedly terrifying," it reported, "The best parts of this novel demand that we take King seriously as a writer with a deeply felt understanding of human psychology." The book had an enormous 1-million-copy first printing and became the latest King best-seller. Besides its paperback edition, the property was popular in an audio-cassette version. In 1990, Kathy Bates and James Caan starred in the film adaptation of *Misery*, directed by Rob Reiner. The thriller earned $61.3 million at the domestic box office and won Bates an Academy Award.

As the 1980s drew to a close, Stephen King had reached a peak of success. Many observers wondered how long the celebrated, fortysomething author could continue his grueling work pace and the flow of his highly commercial output. Little did they know that Stephen had long been grappling with serious personal issues in an effort to keep up with his ever-growing popularity.

7

THE SUMMING UP

By 1985, Stephen King, unknown to his enthusiastic public, was deeply troubled. As he acknowledged later, "I had added drug addiction to my alcohol problems." At the time, he was still in deep denial about his growing range of substance abuse. Although he managed to remain professionally productive through the haze of his addictions, he claimed later to have no recollection of having written *Cujo*. His personal existence was in chaos. His preoccupation with drink and drugs was not only taking a toll on his domestic life; it was ruining his health and spirit. In *On Writing: A Memoir of the Craft* (2000), King describes that, under the influence, he often worked "until midnight with my heart running at a hundred and thirty beats a minute."

In 1986, King's concerned wife Tabitha staged an intervention to shock Stephen into recognizing his path of self-destruction. Calling upon family and friends, she and they confronted Stephen with physical evidence (a huge trash bag filled with beer cans, bags and bottles of drugs, drug paraphernalia, cigarette butts, etc.) of his extensive substance abuse. After the dramatic confrontation, Stephen underwent a gradual realization that all the charges against him were true. Accepting that situation, he feared that if he gave up his severe addictions, he wouldn't be able to write anymore. Nevertheless, he was willing to sacrifice his profession to save his family life.

While coming to grips with his addictions—in itself a harrowing experience—Stephen found the inner will to continue to write, even if, at times, he was deeply dissatisfied with his output. After overcoming his substance abuse, he found—to his great relief—that, with practice, he was soon writing up to his standards without the crutches of drink and drugs.

Getting on with Life

Stephen has long been known for his eccentricities and devotion to the things he likes. For example, each spring when baseball season started and his beloved Boston Red Sox resumed playing, King shaved off his bushy beard. When the sports season ended, Stephen grew another beard. He still loved rock and roll and, being affluent, he could indulge his passion. To insure that he could always

Stephen, a long-time baseball fan, prepares to deliver the first pitch at the Senior League World Series in Bangor, Maine. (Associated Press)

listen to the music he loved while working, he bought a Bangor-based AM radio station, which he redubbed WZON and changed its format to hard rock. Later, when that station's format was changed to all-sports, he acquired another rock station, WKIT.

Although long used to writing on a typewriter, King had kept up with technology and switched to a word processor in the 1980s, just as he would later migrate to a home computer. In this decade, to better define his home life, he moved his business staff to offices near the

Bangor Airport. Because Stephen's acclaim had reached such global proportions, he began to limit his public appearances as he was always being mobbed by over-zealous fans.

In 1987 Stephen suffered a major case of writer's block, which was tied in with his withdrawal from drugs and alcohol. This artistic freeze lasted until May 1988, when his creative juices began to flow again and he demonstrated a new depth to his writing. Meanwhile, he accepted the Bram Stoker Award for his 1987 novel *Misery*. By now, there were an increasing number of published volumes that chronicled Stephen's career and analyzed his tremendous literary output.

The Mature Writer

Having dealt in real life with the creation and destruction of his pen name, Richard Bachman, King took the topic several steps further when he wrote *The Dark Half* (1989), in which a writer's pseudonym develops a murderous life of its own and fights its creator. Many critics considered this well-received book to be King's most personal work. *The Dark Half* was adapted to film in 1993.

After publishing his story "Dolan's Cadillac" in a small press version in 1989, Stephen returned to a major release with his 1990 collection of novellas, *Four Past Midnight*. *The Waste Lands*, the third installment of the sweeping *The Dark Tower* series, appeared in 1991. For many years, several of King's writings had featured the fictional town of Castle Rock, Maine. Deciding it was time to move on to less familiar (and less comfortable) surroundings for upcoming stories, he decided to get rid of the town. He did so in grand fashion in *Needful Things* (1991). In that novel, the focal character, Leland Gaunt, is the devil in disguise, a fiend who craftily manipulates the townsfolk into destroying themselves and their surroundings. In the 1993 feature film version of *Needful Things,* Max Von Sydow effectively took on the leading role.

Besides Annie Wilkes of *Misery,* there had been few memorable female characters in Stephen's extensive writings up to this point. He remedied this in *Gerald's Game* (1992), *Dolores Claibourne* (1992), and *Rose Madder* (1995), a trio of novels that feature strong women as main characters. The most effective of these books is *Dolores Claibourne.* In this uncompromising work, dedicated to his late mother, King explores spousal and child abuse as well as unpleasant aspects of rural life. It is a striking tale of a Maine woman who commits violence in reaction to her drunkard husband's ongoing brutality toward her and their daughter. The 1995 film adaptation of *Dolores Claibourne* was faithful, appropriately grim, and features Kathy Bates (from *Misery*) in the title role.

The Other Sides of Stephen King

When King believes in a cause, not even his concerns about being trapped in an unruly crowd can keep him at home. In 1992, he joined the Rock Bottom Remainders, an amateur band composed largely of writers. (In publishing, *remainders* are books that fail to sell and are then shipped back to the publisher or are sold off at a low price to discount remainder firms.) Among the original members of the group were Stephen (rhythm guitar and occasional vocals), humorist Dave Barry (lead guitar and vocals), cartoonist Matt Groening (backup vocals), author Barbara Kingsolver (keyboard and vocals), writer Michael Dorris (percussion), and author Amy Tan (chorus). The unique group made their first appearance at the American Booksellers Association convention in Anaheim, California. Besides having a good time performing, the group was pleased to donate proceeds from their intermittent concert schedule over the years to charitable causes (such as adult literacy programs).

Also in 1992, the Bangor Chamber of Commerce honored Stephen and Tabitha King for their community service. In receiving the award the couple pointed out, "Whatever we've done for Bangor was the result of what Bangor had done for us." Over the years the Kings gave—and continue to give—substantial charity support to various institutions and public facilities. Among their many

Novelist Amy Tan and Stephen, two members of the rock group the Rock Bottom Remainders (Associated Press)

bequests, they donated a wing to the Bangor Public Library, gave $1.2 million to help with the building of Mansfield Stadium where Bangor Little Leagues games would be played, and heavily endowed scholarships at the University of Maine at Orono and at Milton Academy in Massachusetts.

King experienced another first when he wrote *Sleepwalkers* (1992). Not only was this an original screenplay, it was his first feature-length movie *not* connected to any of his earlier writings. Directed by Mick Garris, the movie is about supernatural newcomers to a Midwestern town. They are sleepwalkers able to change their shapes at will and feed on the life energy of young virgins. While the movie had creative failings, it did boast fun cameos by King, fellow writer Clive Barker, and such genre filmmakers as Tobe Hooper.

Meanwhile, several of King's adapted and original projects continued to be turned into TV offerings. In 1991 there was the ghost tale *Sometimes They Come Back* and *The Golden Years*, which aired on CBS-TV in six parts and dealt with sinister government agencies and individuals fleeing authorities. It was projected to be an ongoing TV series, but failed to find a sufficiently large home audience. In 1993, King wrote an episode of the popular series *The X-Files*, and two years later, he scripted a segment of the revived program, *The Outer Limits*. In 1995, Stephen was represented on the small screen with *The Langoliers*, derived from a novella in his 1990 collection.

Reacquainting Himself with His Public

The year 1993 saw the publication of *Nightmares & Dreamscapes*, King's latest collection of previously published stories. Next came Stephen's complex 1994 novel *Insomnia*, which revolves around an elderly man who experiences his normal sleep routine being dramatically altered by disturbing forces.

Viking, King's hardback publisher of *Insomnia*, urged the author to undertake a major promotional tour for the book. Stephen agreed, but decided to drive his Harley-

Stephen drove his Harley-Davidson motorcycle throughout most of the 1994 promotional tour for his novel Insomnia. (Corbis)

Davidson motorcycle for most portions of the 6,400-mile jaunt across the United States.

Also during 1994, *The Shawshank Redemption* was released. This film is based on King's story "Rita Hayworth and the Shawshank Redemption," part of the 1982 collection *Different Seasons*. Largely set in a prison, it is a very character-driven tale and does not contain the author's trademark supernatural and/or horrific elements. *The Shawshank Redemption* earned seven Academy Award nominations. In addition, the same year, the author won the Bram Stoker Award for his story "Lunch at the Gotham Café." For another yarn, "The Man in the Black Suit," King received both an O. Henry Award and a World Fantasy Award. Both tales appear in his 1997 collection, *Six Stories*.

While 1995 saw the publication of only one new Stephen King book, *Rose Madder*, he was extremely well represented in the marketplace the following year. He had eight new releases in 1996, and they all appeared on the best-sellers list, setting a new industry record. Stephen's 1994 cross-country drive inspired a plot about a menacing evil force named Tak and unsuspecting passengers along Nevada's Highway 50 who are gruesomely done-in by a local sheriff and a troupe of scary creatures. An 11-year-old boy proves to be a worthy opponent of these creepy elements infesting a town called Desperation, Nevada. Making this tale of good versus evil even more intriguing, aspects of the same themes are spun out in two separate books, *Desperation* (authored by King) and *The Regulators* (for which King used his old pen name of Richard Bachman).

Asked why he created the simultaneous publications of these two interlacing works, Stephen explained, "I did it because the Voice told me to do it. Not because I thought it would sell well or because people would like it or because critics would say 'Oh wow' or even 'What a bogus marketing trick.' "

Adding to Stephen's visibility in 1996 was *The Green Mile*, published in six paperback installments released throughout the year. King claimed the concept came about because he was having trouble bringing the plot to its necessary conclusion and felt that the pressure of the serial publication would "be like burning my bridges. I'll have to go on." The story is set in 1932 at Maine's Cold Mountain Penitentiary, where a convict, wrongly sentenced to die for raping and murdering two girls, displays mystical powers. The 1999 feature film adaptation, nominated for four Academy Awards, stars Tom Hanks and Michael Clarke Duncan.

In 1997, not only did King provide readers with a new collection of short yarns (*Six Stories*), he produced the fourth installment of *The Dark Tower* series (*Wizard &*

Glass). Stephen labeled his 1998 novel *Bag of Bones* a "haunted love story." With a nod to Daphne Du Maurier's classic thriller, *Rebecca* (1938), the lead character of this work is a famous writer forced to confront the thorny issue of what gives people's lives humanity and value.

The well-regarded *Bag of Bones* had another distinction: It was King's first book for Scribner, part of the Simon & Schuster publishing empire. Having recently ended his several-year pact with Viking Books over money matters, King's unusual new deal enabled him to take a relatively minimal financial advance against future royalties on book sales in favor of receiving 50 percent of the book's royalties. (In the publishing industry, it is far more standard for an author to receive from 10 to 20 percent of royalties on hardback sales.) As part of the Scribner agreement, which virtually made Stephen a copublisher of his books, other divisions of Simon & Schuster would release the paperback and audio versions of King's new works.

Apt Pupil is a 1998 theatrical feature film based on King's short story of the same name, which appears in the *Different Seasons* collection. Continuing his forays into television, Stephen provided the original teleplay for the ABC-TV miniseries, *Storm of the Century* (1999), for which he served as executive producer and had a cameo as a lawyer. Also that year, King was on the TV quiz show *Jeopardy* and donated his winnings to charity.

A Near Fatal Mishap

In April 1999, King's latest novel, *The Girl Who Loved Tom Gordon,* hit bookstores. Its heroine, a nine-year-old girl lost in the Maine woods, keeps her courage through her adoration of a Boston Red Sox pitcher, whose exploits on the diamond she listens to on the radio. The book is King's tribute to William Golding's *Lord of the Flies* (1954), the one novel Stephen has acknowledged he wishes he had written.

Two months later, on June 19, Stephen was nearly killed in a gory road calamity near his summer house in western Maine. King was taking his daily walk along Route 5 when a minivan driver, distracted by his rottweiler dog in the back seat, lost control of the vehicle. As the van veered off the road, it hit King, tossing him 14 feet. Stephen's severe injuries included broken ribs, multiple fractures of his right hip and leg, a collapsed lung, and assorted contusions to the head. The author was in a far more serious state than news releases revealed, and his recovery required several intricate, painful surgeries and a long recuperation, part of which he spent in Florida.

The driver of the van, 42-year old Bryan Smith, already had a bad driving record. For this latest vehicular mishap, a grand jury indicted Smith on two counts: driving to endanger and aggravated assault. Still, the defendant received a sentence of only six months in jail—which was later dropped—and his driver's license was suspended for only a year. In 2000, several months before his driver's license would have been restored, Smith was found dead in his trailer home. The cause of his death was undetermined and remains so to this day. The whole macabre situation, which seems something out of a Stephen King tale, made an enormous impact on King's life. For a time after his life-changing brush with

Stephen plays with his dog as he recuperates from the June 1999 car accident that almost left him paralyzed. (©Kevin Bennett/Bangor Daily News/The Image Works)

death, Stephen worried if he would ever write again. During this down period, Stephen's *Hearts of Atlantis*, a collection of six stories set in the 1960s, was published in September 1999.

Advice for Fledgling Writers

Resilient and determined, King came back from his near fatal accident by publishing the nonfiction book *On Writing: A Memoir of the Craft* (2000), which he had actually begun writing in 1997.

In *On Writing*, Stephen talks about his many years of experience practicing the writer art and offers sound advice for the new writer of fiction. He suggests, "Skills in description, dialogue, and character development all boil down to seeing or hearing clearly and then transcribing what you see or hear with equal clarity. . . ." King emphasizes that "Story is honorable and trustworthy; plot is shifty, and best kept under house arrest." He advises, "Good fiction always begins with story and progresses to theme; it almost never begins with theme and progresses to story." In the course of his instructional narrative, King disavows that being an author is a glamorous profession. He insists this creative art demands discipline, constant practice, and the ability to shut oneself off from everyday life—even for a few hours—to concentrate on writing.

A Writer for the New Millennium

Taking advantage of ever-improving Internet technology, Stephen experimented with making some of his writings available on the Web. In March 2000 he put his story "Riding the Bullet" online. However, the huge demand by Internet users to retrieve the tale crashed his website. Months later, King offered *The Plant*, a novel which had been privately printed in 1992, as an e-book (that is, text available in electronic format that can be read on the screen of a computer monitor or downloaded to a special portable viewer or printed for hard-copy reading). Stephen planned to release the novel in several 5,000 word e-book segments on the Internet. For each download, the user was requested to send in $1 via mail to a given address. Because fewer than half of those downloading the material followed the author's rules, King abandoned the project.

Stephen returned to new fiction with *Dreamcatcher* (2001), a novel brought to the screen in 2003. Also in 2001, *Black House*, his second collaboration with Peter Straub appeared. In 2002, Stephen published *Everything's Eventual: Fourteen Dark Tales* and the novel *From a Buick Eight*. He continued his popular *The Dark Tower* saga with installment five (*The Wolves of the Calla*) in 2003, followed by part six, *Song of Susannah* (2004), with the final part (*The Dark Tower*) published in fall 2004.

Having often stated in recent years that he planned soon to go into (semi)retirement as a writer (he jokes "I've killed enough of the world's trees"), it remains to be seen if this one-man publishing machine will keep to his goal. It has also been revealed that King suffers from Macular Degeneration, a hereditary disease that could cause the author to go blind at any time. However, the optimist in Stephen says, "At least I'm alive—that's the way I feel about it."

As always, King's works continue to be adapted for the big and small screen. His novella *Secret Window, Secret Garden* became a feature film in 2004, with another novella (*Riding the Bullet*) in movie (pre)production, as are adaptations of his novels *Bag of Bones* and *The Talisman* and the story "Everything's Eventual." His novel *Desperation* is in the works as a TV miniseries. Just as King wrote the TV miniseries *Rose Red* (2002) and characters from that movie were featured in the telefeature *The Diary of Ellen Rimbauer* (2003), so the still workaholic Stephen provided the teleplay adaptation for the upcoming TV miniseries of *Desperation*. He also adapted a 1994 Danish horror-mystery TV miniseries *The Kingdom* into the ABC-TV 15-hour miniseries, *Kingdom Hospital* (2004). Meanwhile, unable to resist the challenge, he accepted a monthly writing assignment—presenting his views on current pop culture—for a recurring one-page feature in *Entertainment Weekly* magazine.

Looking to the Future

From an impoverished and awkward youth to a wealthy, world-famous author, Stephen King has made an impressive journey through life. He admits of his literary career that "I started out as a storyteller. Along the way I became an economic force." He also acknowledges, "People don't read me because they want horror. They read me because they like Stephen King. I've come to that conclusion over the years. . . . I think they come back for the voice more than anything else."

King is proud that he has helped to make horror and supernatural fiction a mainstream genre. He says of his literary specialty, "All writers have a pipeline which goes down into the subconscious. But the man or woman who writes horror stories has a pipeline that goes further, maybe . . . into the sub-subconscious, if you like." On the other hand, he remains modest about his contributions to society. "I have no skill that improves the quality of life in a physical sense at all. The only thing I can do is say: 'Look here, this is the way you didn't look at it before. . . .' I'm like a person who makes eyeglasses for the mind."

From his long experience, King emphasizes that to become a thriving author "is a direct result of conscious

Tabitha and Stephen King, 2003 (Landov)

will. Of course there has to be some talent involved, but talent is a dreadfully cheap commodity, cheaper than table salt. What separates the talented individual from the successful one is a lot of hard work and study; a constant process of honing."

Reflecting on the essential ingredient of good fiction writing, he says, "'It is the tale, not me who tells it.' That's been a good guide to me in life, and I think it would make a good epitaph for my tombstone. Just that and no name."

TIME LINE

1947 Born in Portland, Maine, on September 21

1949 Father, Donald, abandons his family, never to return

1953 After years of moving about the country, Stephen's mother, Ruth, settles with her children in Stratford, Connecticut

1954 Stephen writes his first story: a sci-fi tale about a marauding dinosaur

1958 King family relocates to Durham, Maine

1959 Self-publishes a newspaper, *Dave's Rag*, with his brother and cousin; submits his short stories to publications and receives many rejections

1963 Writes sports articles for the *Lisbon Enterprise*

1965 First story ("I Was a Teenage Grave Robber") accepted for publication by *Comics Review*

1966 Enrolls at the University of Maine at Orono

1967 Makes first professional sale: *Startling Mystery Stories* publishes "The Glass Floor"

1969 Writes his own column ("King's Garbage Truck") for the university newspaper

1970 Graduates from college with a B.A. in English; works at odd jobs (gas station, laundry plant); more of his short stories are accepted for publication

1971 Marries Tabitha Jane Spruce, an aspiring writer, whom he met in college; moves to Herman, Maine; teaches high school classes at nearby Hampden Academy; daughter Naomi is born

1972 Son Joe is born

1973 For a $2,500 advance, *Carrie* is contracted for publication by Doubleday; Ruth King, Stephen's mother, dies

1974 Relocates to Boulder, Colorado; visits the Stanley Hotel, which inspires him to write *The Shining*; Publication: *Carrie*

1975   Settles in Bridgton, Maine; Publication: *'Salem's Lot*

1976   Kirby McCauley becomes King's literary agent; Film: *Carrie*

1977   Son Owen is born; moves to England for three months; buys a house in Center Lovell, Maine; *The Shining* becomes a best-seller, while novel *Rage*—published under pen name of Richard Bachman—passes almost unnoticed

1978   Serves as writer-in-residence at the University of Maine, Orono, teaching four courses; breaks with Doubleday and signs with New American Library; serves as judge for the World Fantasy Awards; Publications: *Night Shift* and *The Stand*

1979   Attends Fifth World Fantasy Convention in Providence, Rhode Island, as guest of honor; Publications: *The Dead Zone* and *The Long Walk* (as Bachman); TV: *'Salem's Lot*

1980   Purchases a Victorian mansion in Bangor, Maine; named Writer of the Year by *People* magazine; Publications: *Firestarter*; Film: *The Shining*

1981   Receives Career Alumni Award from the University of Maine; Publications: *Cujo*, *Danse Macabre*, and *Roadwork* (as Bachman)

1982 Receives the Hugo Award for *Danse Macabre*, the British Fantasy Award for *Cujo*, and World Fantasy Award for "Do the Dead Sing?"; Publications: *Creepshow* (comic format), *The Dark Tower I: The Gunslinger*, *Different Seasons*, and *The Running Man*; Film: *Creepshow* (in which he has a role)

1983 Purchases Bangor radio station, renaming it WZON; Publications: *Christine*, and *Pet Sematary*. Films: *Christine*, *Cujo*, and *The Dead Zone*

1984 Publications: *Cycle of the Werewolf*, *The Eyes of the Dragon*, *The Talisman* (with Peter Straub), and *Thinner* (as Bachman). Films: *Children of the Corn* and *Firestarter*; TV: *Tales from the Darkside* (episode)

1985 After years of rumors, it is publicly confirmed that Richard Bachman is pseudonym of King; debut issue of *Castle Rock*, the King newsletter; five of King's books appear on national best-seller lists at the same time, a record for any author so far. Publications: *Skeleton Crew*; Films: *Cat's Eye* and *Silver Bullet*; TV: The *Twilight Zone* (episode)

1986 Publications: *It*; Films: *Maximum Overdrive* (director), *Stand by Me*

1987 Achieves sobriety; suffers a writer's block; Publications: *The Dark Tower II: The Drawing of the*

Three, Misery, and *The Tommyknockers*; Films: *Creepshow 2* and *The Running Man*; TV: *A Return to 'Salem's Lot*

1988   Receives the Bram Stoker Award for *Misery*

1989   Gives donation to Milton Academy in Massachusetts, whose arts and music center is renamed after King's mother, Ruth; donates funds for renovation work at the public library in Old Town, Maine; Publication: *The Dark Half*; Film: *Pet Sematary*

1990   "Head Down," his account of a Little League team enjoying a championship season, is published by the *New Yorker*; Publications: *Four Past Midnight* and *The Stand* (unabridged edition); Films: *Graveyard Shift* and *Misery*; TV: *It*

1991   Publications: *The Dark Tower III: The Waste Lands*, and *Needful Things*; Films: *Children of the Corn II: The Final Sacrifice*; TV: *Golden Years* and *Sometimes They Come Back*

1992   Stephen and Tabitha King receive an award for community service to Bangor; helps found and performs with Rock Bottom Remainders band; Publications: *Gerald's Game* and *The Plant*; Films: *The Lawnmower Man*, *Pet Sematary II*, and *Sleepwalkers*

1993 Publications: *Dolores Claiborne* and *Nightmares & Dreamscapes*; Films: *The Dark Half* and *Needful Things*; TV: *The Tommyknockers* and *The X-Files* (episode)

1994 Undertakes first national book tour in several years, promoting *Insomnia*; wins Bram Stoker Award for "Lunch at the Gotham Café" and a World Fantasy Award for "The Man in the Black Suit"; Publications: *Insomnia*; Films: *Children of the Corn III* and *The Shawshank Redemption*; TV: *The Stand*

1995 Publications: *Rose Madder*; Films: *Dolores Claiborne* and *The Mangler*; TV: *The Langoliers* and *The Outer Limits* (episode)

1996 Has six books on the best-seller list; receives O. Henry Award for "The Man in the Black Suit" Publications: *Desperation, The Green Mile* (in six-part serial novel format), and *The Regulators* (as Bachman); Films: *Children of the Corn IV: The Gathering, Thinner*, and *Sometimes They Come Back . . . Again*

1997 Publications: *The Dark Tower IV: Wizard & Glass* and *Six Stories*; Films: *The Night Flier* (premiered earlier on cable TV); TV: *Quicksilver Highway* and *Stephen King's The Shining* (remake)

1998 Makes new publishing pact with Scribner/Simon & Schuster; Publications: *Bag of Bones*; Films: *Apt Pupil, Children of the Corn V: Fields of Terror,* and *Trucks*

1999 Severely injured in car accident while walking along a Maine highway. Publications: *The Girl Who Loved Tom Gordon, Hearts in Atlantis,* and *Storm of the Century*; Films: *Children of the Corn 666: Isaac's Return* and *The Green Mile*; TV: *The Golden Years II* and *Storm of the Century*

2000 "Riding the Bullet" and *The Plant* are published on the Internet. Publication: *On Writing*; Film: *Paranoid*

2001 Publications: *Black House* (with Peter Straub) and *Dreamcatcher*; Films: *Children of the Corn 7: Revelation, Hearts in Atlantis,* and *The Mangler 2*

2002 Revealed that King suffers from a degenerate eye condition; Publications: *Everything's Eventual: 14 Dark Tales* and *From a Buick Eight*; TV: *Carrie* and *Rose Red*

2003 Receives National Book Award for distinguished contribution to American letters; writes monthly column for *Entertainment Weekly*; Publications: *The Dark Tower V: The Wolves of the Calla*; Films: *Dreamcatcher*

2004 Publications: *The Dark Tower VI: Song of Susannah* and *The Dark Tower VII: The Dark Tower*. Films: *Bag of Bones, Everything's Eventual, Riding the Bullet, Secret Window,* and *The Talisman*; TV: *Desperation* (miniseries)

HOW TO BECOME A WRITER

THE JOB

Writers work in the field of communications. They deal with the written word, whether it is destined for the printed page, broadcast, computer screen, or live theater. The nature of their work is as varied as the materials they produce: books, magazines, trade journals, newspapers, technical reports, company newsletters and other publications, advertisements, speeches, scripts for motion picture and stage productions, and scripts for radio and television broadcast. Writers develop ideas and write for all media.

Prose writers for newspapers, magazines, and books share many of the same duties. First they come up with an idea for an article or book from their own interests or are assigned a topic by an editor. The topic is of relevance to the particular publication; for example, a writer for a magazine on parenting may be assigned an article on car seat safety. Then writers begin gathering as much information as possible about the subject through library research, interviews, the Internet, observation, and other methods. They keep extensive notes from which they will draw material for their project. Once the material has been organized and arranged in logical sequence, writers prepare a written outline. The process of developing a piece of writing is exciting, although it can also involve detailed and solitary work. After researching an idea, a writer might discover that a different perspective or related topic would be more effective, entertaining, or marketable.

When working on an assignment, writers often submit their outlines to a literary agent, an editor, or a publishing company representative for approval. Then they write a first draft of the manuscript, trying to put the material into words that will have the desired effect on their audience. They rewrite and polish sections of the material as they proceed, always searching for just the right way of imparting information or expressing an idea or opinion. A manuscript may be reviewed, corrected, and revised numerous times before a final copy is submitted. Even after that, an editor may request additional changes.

Writers for newspapers, magazines, or books often specialize in their subject matter. Some writers might have an educational background that allows them to give critical interpretations or analyses. For example, a health or science writer for a newspaper typically has a degree in biology and can interpret new ideas in the field for the average reader.

Columnists or *commentators* analyze news and social issues. They write about events from the standpoint of their own experience or opinion. *Critics* review literary, musical, or artistic works and performances. *Editorial writers* write on topics of public interest, and their comments, consistent with the viewpoints and policies of their employers, are intended to stimulate or mold public opinion. *Newswriters* work for newspapers, radio, or TV news departments, writing news stories from notes supplied by reporters or wire services.

Corporate writers and writers for nonprofit organizations have a wide variety of responsibilities. These writers may work in such places as a large insurance corporation or a small nonprofit religious group, where they may be required to write news releases, annual reports, speeches for the company head, or public relations materials. Typically, they are assigned a topic with length requirements for a given project. They may receive raw research materials, such as statistics, and they are expected to conduct additional research, including personal interviews. These writers must be able to write quickly and accurately on short deadlines, while also working with people whose primary job is not in the communications field. The written work is submitted to a supervisor, and often a legal department, for approval; rewrites are a normal part of this job.

Copywriters write copy primarily designed to sell goods and services. Their work appears as advertisements in newspapers, magazines, and other publications or as commercials on radio and television broadcasts. Sales and marketing representatives first provide information on the product and help determine the style and length of the copy. The copywriters conduct additional research and interviews; to formulate an effective approach, they study advertising trends and review surveys of consumer preferences. Armed with this information, copywriters write a draft that is submitted to the account executive and the client for approval. The copy is often returned for correction and revision until everyone involved is satisfied. Copywriters, like corporate writers, may also write articles, bulletins, news releases, sales letters, speeches, and other related informative and promotional material. Many copywriters are employed in advertising agencies. They also may work for public relations firms or in communications departments of large companies.

Technical writers can be divided into two main groups: those who convert technical information into material for the general public and those who convey technical information among professionals. Technical writers in the first group may prepare service manuals or handbooks, instruction or repair booklets, or sales literature or brochures; those in the second group may write grant proposals, research reports, contract specifications, or research abstracts.

Screenwriters prepare scripts for motion pictures or television. They select, or are assigned, a subject, conduct research, write and submit a plot outline and narrative synopsis (treatment), and confer with the producer and/or director about possible revisions. Screenwriters may adapt books or plays for film and television dramatizations. They often collaborate with other screenwriters and may specialize in a particular type of script or writing.

Playwrights do similar writing for the stage. They write dialogue and describe action for plays that may be tragedies, comedies, or dramas, with themes sometimes adapted from fictional, historical, or narrative sources. Playwrights combine the elements of action, conflict, purpose, and resolution to depict events from real or imaginary life. They often make revisions even while the play is in rehearsal.

Continuity writers prepare the material read by radio and television announcers to introduce or connect various parts of their programs.

Novelists and *short story writers* create stories that may be published in books, magazines, or literary journals. They take incidents from their own lives, from news events, or from their imaginations and create characters, settings, actions, and resolutions. *Poets* create narrative, dramatic, or lyric poetry for books, magazines, or other publications, as well as for special events such as commemorations. These writers may work with literary agents or editors who help guide them through the writing process, which includes research of the subject matter and an understanding of the intended audience. Many universities and colleges offer graduate degrees in creative writing. In these programs, students work intensively with published writers to learn the art of storytelling.

Writers can be employed either as in-house staff or as freelancers. Pay varies according to experience and the position, but freelancers must provide their own office space and equipment such as computers and fax machines. Freelancers also are responsible for keeping tax records, sending out invoices, negotiating contracts, and providing their own health insurance.

REQUIREMENTS

High School

While in high school, build a broad educational foundation by taking courses in English, literature, foreign languages, general science, social studies, computer science, and typing. The ability to type is almost a requisite for all positions in the communications field, as is familiarity with computers.

Postsecondary Training

Competition for writing jobs almost always demands the background of a college education. Many employers prefer that you have a broad liberal arts background or majors in English, literature, history, philosophy, or one of the social sciences. Other employers desire communications or journalism training in college. Occasionally, a master's degree in a specialized writing field may be required. A number of schools offer courses in journalism, and some of them offer courses or majors in book publishing, publication management, and newspaper and magazine writing.

In addition to formal coursework, most employers look for practical writing experience. If you have served on high school or college newspapers, yearbooks, or literary magazines, you will make a better candidate, as well as if you have worked for small community newspapers or radio stations, even in an unpaid position. Many book publishers, magazines, newspapers, and radio and television stations have summer internship programs that provide valuable training if you want to learn about the publishing and broadcasting businesses. Interns do many simple tasks, such as running errands and answering phones, but some may be asked to perform research, conduct interviews, or even write some minor pieces.

Writers who specialize in technical fields may need degrees, concentrated course work, or experience in specific subject areas. This applies frequently to engineering, business, or one of the sciences. Also, technical communications is a degree now offered at many universities and colleges.

If you wish to enter positions with the federal government, you will have to take a civil service examination and meet certain specified requirements, according to the type and level of position.

Other Requirements

To be a writer, you should be creative and able to express ideas clearly, have a broad general knowledge, be skilled in research techniques, and be computer literate. Other assets include curiosity, persistence, initiative, resourcefulness, and an accurate memory. For some jobs—on a newspaper, for example, where the activity is hectic and deadlines are short—the ability to concentrate and produce under pressure is essential.

EXPLORING

As a high school or college student, you can test your interest and aptitude in the field of writing by serving as a reporter or writer on school newspapers, yearbooks, and literary magazines. Various writing courses and workshops will offer you the opportunity to sharpen your writing skills.

Small community newspapers and local radio stations often welcome contributions from outside sources, although they may not have the resources to pay for them. Jobs in bookstores, magazine shops, and newsstands provide a chance to become familiar with various publications.

You can also obtain information on writing as a career by visiting local newspapers, publishers, or radio and television stations and interviewing some of the writers who work there. Career conferences and other guidance programs frequently include speakers on the entire field of communications from local or national organizations.

EMPLOYERS

There are approximately 126,000 writers and authors, and 57,000 technical writers, currently employed in the United States. Nearly a fourth of salaried writers and editors work for newspapers, magazines, and book publishers, according to the *Occupational Outlook Handbook*. Writers are also employed by advertising agencies and public relations firms, in radio and television broadcasting, and for journals and newsletters published by business and nonprofit organizations, such as professional associations, labor unions, and religious organizations. Other employers are government agencies and film production companies.

STARTING OUT

A fair amount of experience is required to gain a high-level position in the field. Most writers start out in entry-level positions. These jobs may be listed with college placement offices, or they may be obtained by applying directly to the employment departments of the individual publishers or broadcasting companies. Graduates who previously served internships with these companies often have the advantage of knowing someone who can give them a personal recommendation. Want ads in newspapers and trade journals are another source for jobs. Because of the competition for positions, however, few vacancies are listed with public or private employment agencies.

Employers in the communications field usually are interested in samples of published writing. These are often assembled in an organized portfolio or scrapbook. Bylined or signed articles are more credible (and, as a result, more useful) than stories whose source is not identified.

Beginning positions as a junior writer usually involve library research, preparation of rough drafts for part or all of a report, cataloging, and other related writing tasks. These are generally carried on under the supervision of a senior writer.

Some technical writers have entered the field after working in public relations departments or as technicians or research assistants, then transferring to technical writing as openings occur. Many firms now hire writers directly upon application or recommendation of college professors and placement offices.

Establishing yourself as a full-time novelist is very difficult. Most successful authors start by writing in their free time while relying on a full-time position to pay for their living expenses. Although a full-time position in a writing-related position enables you to hone your writing skills, some authors find that working in a nonwriting field keeps their creative energy in reserve. This helps them focus on writing and submitting works for publication in their free time.

ADVANCEMENT

Most writers find their first jobs as editorial or production assistants. Advancement may be more rapid in small companies, where beginners learn by doing a bit of every-thing and may be given writing tasks immediately. In large firms, duties are usually more compartmentalized. Assistants in entry-level positions are assigned such tasks as research, fact checking, and copyrighting, but it gener-ally takes much longer to advance to full-scale writing duties.

Promotion into more responsible positions may come with the assignment of more important articles and sto-ries to write, or it may be the result of moving to another company. Mobility among employees in this field is com-mon. An assistant in one publishing house may switch to an executive position in another. Or a writer may switch to a related field as a type of advancement.

A technical writer can be promoted to positions of responsibility by moving from such jobs as writer to tech-nical editor to project leader or documentation manager. Opportunities in specialized positions also are possible.

Freelance or self-employed writers earn advancement in the form of larger fees as they gain exposure and estab-lish their reputations.

EARNINGS

In 2001, median annual earnings for salaried writers and authors were $42,450 a year, according to the Bureau of Labor Statistics. The lowest 10 percent earned less than

$20,570, while the highest 10 percent earned $83,180 or more. In book publishing, some specialties pay better than others. Technical writers earned a median salary of $49,370 in 2001.

In addition to their salaries, many writers earn income from freelance work. Part-time freelancers may earn from $5,000 to $15,000 a year. Freelance earnings vary widely. Full-time established freelance writers may earn up to $75,000 a year.

WORK ENVIRONMENT

Working conditions vary for writers. Although their workweek usually runs 35–40 hours, many writers work overtime. A publication issued frequently has more deadlines closer together, creating greater pressures to meet them. The work is especially hectic on newspapers and at broadcasting companies, which operate seven days a week. Writers often work nights and weekends to meet deadlines or to cover a late-developing story.

Most writers work independently, but they often must cooperate with artists, photographers, rewriters, and advertising people who may have widely differing ideas of how the materials should be prepared and presented.

Physical surroundings range from comfortable private offices to noisy, crowded newsrooms filled with other workers typing and talking on the telephone. Some writers must confine their research to the library or telephone interviews, but others may travel to other cities or countries or to local sites, such as theaters, ballparks, airports, factories, or other offices.

The work is arduous, but most writers are seldom bored. Some jobs, such as that of the foreign correspondent, require travel. The most difficult element is the continual pressure of deadlines. People who are the most content as writers enjoy and work well with deadline pressure.

OUTLOOK

The employment of writers is expected to increase faster than the average rate of all occupations over the next several years, according to the U.S. Department of Labor. The demand for writers by newspapers, periodicals, book publishers, and nonprofit organizations is expected to increase. The growth of online publishing on company websites and other online services will also demand many talented writers; those with computer skills will be at an advantage as a result. Advertising and public relations will also provide job opportunities.

The major book and magazine publishers, broadcasting companies, advertising agencies, public relations firms, and the federal government account for the concentration of writers in large cities such as New York,

Chicago, Los Angeles, Boston, Philadelphia, San Francisco, and Washington, D.C. Opportunities with small newspapers, corporations, and professional, religious, business, technical, and trade publications can be found throughout the country.

People entering this field should realize that the competition for jobs is extremely keen. Beginners may especially have difficulty finding employment. Of the thousands who graduate each year with degrees in English, journalism, communications, and the liberal arts and intend to establish a career as a writer, many turn to other occupations when they find that applicants far outnumber the job openings available. College students would do well to keep this in mind and prepare for an unrelated alternate career in the event they are unable to obtain a position as writer; another benefit of this approach is that, at the same time, they will become qualified as writers in a specialized field. The practicality of preparing for alternate careers is borne out by the fact that opportunities are best in firms that prepare business and trade publications and in technical writing.

Potential writers who end up working in a different field may be able to earn some income as freelancers, selling articles, stories, books, and possibly TV and movie scripts, but it is usually difficult for anyone to be self-supporting entirely on independent writing.

TO LEARN MORE ABOUT WRITERS AND WRITING

BOOKS

Arana, Marie, Ed. *The Writing Life: Writers on How They Think and Work. A Collection from the Washington Post Book World.* New York: PublicAffairs, 2003.

Cowden, Tami D., Caro LaFever, and Sue Viders. *The Complete Writer's Guide to Heroes and Heroines.* Los Angeles: Lone Eagle Publishing Company, 2000.

Gardner, John. *The Art of Fiction: Notes on Craft for Young Writers.* Vintage, 1991.

Goldberg, Natalie. *Writing Down the Bones: Freeing the Writer Within.* Boston, Mass.: Shambhala, 1986.

Van Belkom, Edo. *Writing Horror.* Self Counsel Press, 2000.

Zinsser, William K. *On Writing Well: The Classic Guide to Writing Nonfiction.* New York: HarperResource, 2001.

ORGANIZATIONS AND WEBSITES

For information on writing and editing careers in the field of communications, contact

National Association of Science Writers

PO Box 890

Hedgesville, WV 25427

Tel: 304-754-5077

http://www.nasw.org

This organization offers student memberships for those interested in opinion writing.

National Conference of Editorial Writers

3899 North Front Street

Harrisburg, PA 17110

Tel: 717-703-3015

Email: ncew@pa-news.org

http://www.ncew.org

The following website is a great source of information on the writing industry, including helpful advice from editors, agents, and writers of all kinds. Here you can also order the most recent edition of *Writer's Market,* an annual publication that lists contact information for thousands of publishing companies, agents, and magazines. http://www.writersmarket.com

TO LEARN MORE ABOUT STEPHEN KING

BOOKS

Beahm, George. *Stephen King: America's Best-Loved Boogeyman.* Kansas City, Mo. : Andrews McMeel, 1998.

———. *Stephen King: A to Z.* Kansas City, Mo.: Andrews McMeel, 1998.

———. *Stephen King Country.* Philadelphia: Running Press, 1999.

Bloom, Harold, ed. *Bloom's BioCritiques: Stephen King.* Philadelphia: Chelsea House, 2002.

Jones, Stephen. *Creepshows: The Illustrated Stephen King Movie Guide.* New York: Billboard, 2002.

Keyishian, Amy, and Marjorie Keyishian. *Stephen King.* New York: Chelsea House, 1996.*

King, Stephen. *Danse Macabre*. New York: Berkeley, 1981.

———. *On Writing: A Memoir of the Craft*. New York: Scribner, 2000.

Magistrale, Tony. *Hollywood's Stephen King*. London: Palgrave Macmillan, 2003.

Russell, Sharon A. *Stephen King: A Critical Companion*. Westport, Conn.: Greenwood, 1996.

Saidman, Anne. *Stephen King: Master of Horror*. Minneapolis: Lerner Publications, 1992.*

Spignesi, Stephen J., Ed.. *The Complete Stephen King Encyclopedia*. Chicago: Contemporary Books, 1991.

———. *The Essential Stephen King*. Franklin Lakes, N.J.: New Page, 2003.

Underwood, Tim, and Chuck Miller, eds. *Bare Bones*. San Diego, Calif.: Lucent Books, 1999.

———. *Feast of Fear*. New York: Warner, 1989.

Wiater, Stanley, and Christopher Golden and Hank Wagner. *The Stephen King Universe: A Guide to the Worlds of the King of Horror*. Los Angeles: Renaissance, 2001.

Wilson, Suzan. *Stephen King: King of Thrillers and Horror*. Berkeley Heights, N.J.: Enslow, 2000.*

Wukovits, John F. *Stephen King*. San Diego, Calif.: Lucent Books, 1999.*

* Young Adult Book

WEBSITES

An Absolute Guide to Stephen King

http://www.stephenkingnews.com/

Internet Movie Database

http://www.imdb.com

King of Horror

http://www.acay.com.au/ ~ normab/king/king-1.htm

The Official Stephen King Web Presence

http://www.stephenking.com

Simon Says

http://www.simonsays.com/subs/index.cfm?areaid = 21

Stephen King Net

http://www.stephen-king.net

Stephen King Tribute

http://www.malakoff.com/sking.htm

The Stephen King Website

http://home.pacbell.net/jepace/king.html

Stephen King's Room

http://users.qnet.com/ ~ raven//skroom.html

INDEX

Page numbers in *italics* indicate illustrations.

L

ABOUT THE AUTHOR

James Robert Parish, a former entertainment reporter, publicist, and book series editor, is the author of many published biographies and reference books of the entertainment industry including *Steven Spielberg: Filmmaker*; *Tom Hanks: Actor*; *Whitney Houston*; *The Hollywood Book of Love*; *Hollywood Divas*; *Hollywood Bad Boys*; *The Encyclopedia of Ethnic Groups in Hollywood*; *Jet Li*; *Jason Biggs*; *Gus Van Sant*; *The Hollywood Book of Death*; *Whoopi Goldberg*; *Rosie O'Donnell's Story*; *The Unofficial "Murder, She Wrote" Casebook*; *Let's Talk! America's Favorite TV Talk Show Hosts*; *Liza Minnelli*; *The Elvis Presley Scrapbook*; and *Hollywood's Great Love Teams*.

Mr. Parish is a frequent on-camera interviewee on cable and network TV for documentaries on the performing arts both in the United States and in the United Kingdom. He resides in Studio City, California.